Critical Guides to Spanish Texts

G000041454

EDITED BY J. E. VAREY AND A. D. DEYERMOND

Critical Guides to Spanish Texts

13 San Juan de la Cruz: Poems

SAN JUAN DE LA CRUZ

Poems

Margaret Wilson

Senior Lecturer in Spanish in the
University of Hull

Grant & Cutler Ltd *in association with*
Tamesis Books Ltd 1975

© Grant & Cutler Ltd
   1975
ISBN 0 900411 94 5

I.S.B.N. 84-399-3862-4

DEPÓSITO LEGAL: V. 2.427 - 1975

Printed in Spain by
Artes Gráficas Soler, S.A., Valencia
for
GRANT AND CUTLER LTD
11, BUCKINGHAM STREET, LONDON, W.C.2.

Contents

I   Introduction   7

II   Mysticism   17

III   Minor Non-mystical Poems   25

IV   Minor Mystical Poems   35

V   Major Poems: *Noche oscura* and *Llama de amor viva*   45

VI   Major Poems: *Cántico espiritual*   55

VII   Conclusion   69

Bibliographical Note   77

Prefatory Note

The poems of San Juan de la Cruz are available in many editions, but nearly always in conjunction with the commentaries, or with a translation, or appended to works of criticism; there is no standard edition of the poems alone. In quoting from the poems I have followed the text given by P. Lucinio del SS. Sacramento in *Vida y obras de San Juan de la Cruz,* Biblioteca de Autores Cristianos, 4th ed., Madrid, 1960 (item *1* in the Bibliographical Note at the end of this study); but where so small a number of poems is concerned there should be no problem of identification for readers using other editions.

References to works listed in the Bibliographical Note are indicated by the appropriate numeral in italics, thus: (*12,* pp. 276–8).

I am very grateful to Professors A. D. Deyermond and J. E. Varey, the editors of this series, for a number of helpful suggestions for the improvement of my text.

I *Introduction*

One of the many distinctions which the Romantic movement brought into focus was that between public and private poetry. Until the late eighteenth century the writing of literature was governed by the notion of decorum: just as a particular social occasion may call for a certain mode of dress, so it was accepted that subject-matter must be appropriate to genre, and style to subject-matter. Some writers of the post-Renaissance period, Góngora and Quevedo for example, bent the rules deliberately on occasion in order to shock; but such an effect depended necessarily on the existence of those rules. Complete permissiveness precludes the possibility of shock; and permissiveness in literature is a very modern phenomenon. Moreover, just as decorum in dress is a social norm, and implies that one's garments are going to be seen and judged by others, so the existence of rules for literature presupposed a public, a community of readers, whose approval mattered to an author, and who would be the ultimate arbiters of what was written. Naturally all poets who publish their work still hope to have it read, and presumably to make money out of it; but they are not usually thought nowadays to be writing primarily with an audience in mind. Since the early nineteenth century poetry, like most of the other arts, has been conceived of first and foremost as the artist's self-expression; has become private, in fact. It was by no means always so.

One of the reasons why much lyric poetry in the sixteenth century, for instance, was public, as drama must always be public, was that it had a very similar social function: that of entertainment. People then depended very largely on such diversions as they could provide for themselves, and in aristocratic circles one of the chief of these was the recital of songs, often with words from the courtiers' own pens. Musical settings to some of the poems of Garcilaso de la Vega still exist in contemporary song-books. They must often have been performed at court; and for this purpose the fact that his love poetry seems to be the genuine expression of intense emotion, while

that of his friend Boscán rings rather hollow, was of little importance.
Garcilaso himself, still holding back certain secrets from his poems
despite his outpouring of feeling, implicitly acknowledges that he
has a public in view:

> Canción, yo he dicho más que me mandaron,
> y menos que pensé;
> no me pregunten más, que lo diré. *(Canción segunda)*

There is however one sphere of poetry that differs somewhat from
the rest: that of the religious lyric. Here it is possible to make a
distinction between those poems directed to an audience, or at least
written with readers in mind, and others which appear to have originated as pure self-expression. An heroic ode like Herrera's great
Canción por la victoria de Lepanto, with its rhetoric, its exhort-
ations and its mood of national fervour, is clearly public in every
sense. Even the poets of the religious orders often had their audience, if a more restricted one: the members of their own communities, among whom, as in the society of the court, the writing of
verse and the singing of songs constituted a legitimate diversion.
The role of poetry and song in the life and devotions of the Carmelite
Order has been well studied by Emilio Orozco *(15,* pp. 115–70);
and it can be easily illustrated from the poems of Santa Teresa.
When a new nun was to be professed, Teresa would modify a rustic
wedding song for the occasion:

> ¡Oh dichosa tal zagala
> que hoy se ha dado a un tal Zagal!
>
> (Santa Teresa de Jesús, *Obras com-
> pletas,* Madrid, Aguilar, 1945, p.729)

She would celebrate Easter with a hymn clearly intended to be sung
in procession, if not actually danced to:

> Hoy ha vencido un guerrero
> al mundo y sus valedores.
> ¡Vuelta, vuelta, pecadores,
> sigamos este sendero!   (p.726)

And even when her nuns' new coarse woollen habits were found to
harbour fleas, it was with a song that she met the situation, invoking
heavenly aid:

> Pues nos dais vestido nuevo,
>   Rey celestial,
> librad de la mala gente
>   este sayal.   (p.730)

Others of Teresa's verses, however, seem to have issued solely from her own inner experiences:

> Vivo ya fuera de mí,
> después que muero de amor;
> porque vivo en el Señor,
> que me quiso para sí;   (p.717)

and the same is true of nearly all the more memorable poems of both Fray Luis de León and San Juan de la Cruz: poems full of personal longing, personal anguish or personal ecstasy, some of which, in the case of both men, were actually composed in the enforced privacy of solitary confinement.

Among the poems of San Juan it is not difficult to distinguish the private and personal from the more objective. His ten *Romances,* nine of them constituting a sequence on the Creation and the Incarnation, are quite impersonal. Along with the form of the medieval ballad they perpetuate its naivety, and they give the impression of having been written with the edification of others in mind, others less advanced in spiritual development than the poet himself. The *Pastorcico,* although more lyrical and more polished, similarly focuses on the figure of Christ, and clearly envisages a reader in whom it aims to induce a devotional response; it too therefore belongs to his public poetry. His remaining poems are very different, being all about himself. They are full of first-person pronouns and verbs. They chronicle his spiritual life, and more particularly his experiences of mystical union with God; and they presuppose no reader. The mystical experience seems to be the most intimate known to man, and these poems are among the most private ever written. This distinguishes them from the bulk of Golden Age verse, and suggests that from one point of view at least they may find an easier response from modern readers who look to poetry for an account of personal experience.

The distinction between the public and the private does not correspond in the case of San Juan to any difference in circumstances of composition, or in the subsequent history of the poems themselves. Most of the known facts of his life are recorded in depositions made by his associates, either to his first biographer or in connection with the process for his beatification; and from such contemporary testimonies it appears that his most fruitful period as a poet was his nine-month imprisonment in Toledo at the age of 35. Because of his collaboration with Santa Teresa in the reform of the Carmelite Order, he had fallen foul of that branch of the Order which resisted reform and was content with a less strict observance of the monastic rule. On the night of December 3rd 1577 a band of these Mitigated Carmelites abducted Fray Juan de la Cruz, as he then was, from the convent of the Encarnación in Avila and took him to their monastery in Toledo, where he was held prisoner, in conditions of extreme physical privation, until the following August. There it was that he composed the greater part of his longest poem, the *Canciones entre el alma y el Esposo,* or *Cántico espiritual*; the *Fonte que mana y corre*; probably the *Noche oscura*; and also the *Romances*. It is perhaps significant that it was the *Romances* that he chose to recite, the day after his daring escape, to the Reformed Carmelite nuns of Toledo in whose convent he had taken refuge.

Some little time later, however, when he is once more settled as confessor to a house of the Reform, this time at Beas in the southeast, he also uses his mystical poems as teaching material. So difficult do the nuns find them that they ask for expositions of what the poems are intended to convey; that is, for the private material to be made public. Thus the great theological treatises come into being, as commentaries on the three major poems. The *Cántico espiritual* and *Llama de amor viva* follow the texts of their respective poems stanza by stanza; the *Noche oscura* and *Subida del Monte Carmelo* both expound the poem "En una noche oscura", but in a more general manner. The exegeses are the work of the spiritual director rather than the poet; and although they were written only a few years after their poems, and seem from the start to have circulated with them as part of the same work — hence the difficulty of finding different titles to distinguish between poems and commentary — the author does appear at times to be reading in allegorical meanings, or even occasionally falsifying the sense of what he originally wrote. They are not therefore the infallible guides that an author's exposition of his own writings might be expected to be; but any serious student of the poems must obviously consult them.

San Juan's writings all remained unpublished for some forty-odd years, during which time they circulated among Carmelite houses in manuscript copies. None of the extant MSS is in the author's own hand, and since there are considerable variations between them questions of authenticity arise. The most perplexing of these concern the *Cántico espiritual,* the different versions of which have provoked vigorous debate from the 1920s onwards. Dr Roger Duvivier has recently given what is probably the fullest and clearest exposition of the problems (*17,* pp.xxxi–lxxix). Stated as simply as possible, the position is that the *Cántico* (poem plus commentary) exists in three main versions, which have been designated A, A¹ and B. Version A is that of the first edition (Brussels, 1627), and is authenticated by a manuscript belonging to the Carmelites of Sanlúcar de Barrameda. This manuscript is not in San Juan's own hand, but bears some corrections and marginal annotations which almost certainly are. Version A¹, that of the first Spanish edition (Madrid, 1630), differs from A only in minor respects. Version B, however, alters the order of some of the stanzas of the poem, and considerably lengthens the commentary, slanting the direction of the latter away from those mystical states achieved only by the spiritual élite, and towards more generalized devotional instruction. It exists in a manuscript belonging to the Carmelites of Jaén, and first became widely known in 1701 when this was used for a new edition of the Saint's works, published in Seville. From then on it became the official version of the *Cántico,* supplanting A and A¹ which for two centuries were virtually lost from sight. Twentieth-century critics have revalidated A, but disagree about the authenticity of B. Many Spanish scholars, including some who are themselves Carmelites, hold that B is San Juan's own reworking of his earlier poem and treatise; and this view is given some support by the fact that the marginal annotations of the Sanlúcar manuscript seem to have provided the basis for some of the elaborations of B. Their opponents, headed by Frenchmen, dismiss B as a distortion of the original by later theologians who were out of sympathy with the mysticism of San Juan.

The question is still by no means settled, and perhaps never will be. Fortunately it is not of major importance for the understanding of the poem alone, since the order of the stanzas does not greatly affect its sense or its aesthetic qualities. But as in order to analyse the poem at all a choice must be made, I shall in the relevant chapter of this study follow Version A, chiefly because the commentary in this version seems to be a better guide. It has a greater sense of immediacy, and must at least be closer in time to the poem it expounds.

The student of San Juan the poet also faces another question of authenticity: that of which poems constitute the genuine canon. This problem, in contrast to those of the *Cántico,* has received little attention; a fact symptomatic of the far greater interest aroused by San Juan as a theologian than as a poet. By any reckoning his extant poems are few. In addition to the *Cántico* the Sanlúcar manuscript contains the *Noche oscura,* the *Llama de amor viva,* the *Pastorcico, La fonte que mana y corre,* the ten *Romances,* and three poems in octosyllabic metre each glossing an *estribillo* (initial short stanza) in the manner of the traditional *canción* or *villancico*: "Entréme donde no supe", "Vivo sin vivir en mí", and "Tras de un amoroso lance". These eighteen poems would thus seem to be authenticated by the fact that the manuscript almost certainly passed through the author's hands. The Jaén manuscript, which lacks this authority, includes two further glosses, "Sin arrimo y con arrimo" and "Por toda la hermosura"; and certain other manuscripts credit San Juan with two additional poems, "Del agua de la vida" and "Si de mi baja suerte", both in the same *lira* metre as the *Cántico* (that is, stanzas of five lines of 7, 11, 7, 7, 11 syllables respectively, rhyming a b a b b). There are therefore four poems of questionable authorship.

The Jaén glosses seem to be so similar to the other three poems of this type, and so full of San Juan's characteristic imagery and vocabulary, that it would surely be perverse not to admit them as his. Of the doubtful *lira* poems, however, Dámaso Alonso is unquestionably right in saying that "el análisis de su estilo no parece en modo alguno autorizar su atribución al Santo" (2, p. 11). It may be thought that stylistic criteria are unreliable in the case of a poet who can write verses as dissimilar as the *Romances* and the *Cántico*; and it is true that, without supporting evidence, the former would not be recognized as the work of the great mystic. But there is a

big difference between their deliberate naivety and the fatuity of
lines like:

> ¿Oh cuándo, amor, oh cuándo,
> cuándo tengo de verme en tanta gloria?
> ¿Cuándo será este cuándo?
> ¿Cuándo de aquesta escoria
> saliendo alcanzaré tan gran victoria?

While this is admittedly the worst stanza in the two *lira* poems,
there are no others of any real merit to redeem it. These poems may
be read in the Austral edition of *Obras escogidas* of San Juan, which
includes them without any discussion of their authorship. I prefer
to follow Dámaso Alonso in accepting as authentic only those twenty
poems which he offers as the *Poesías completas* in his Crisol edition
already referred to.

Dámaso Alonso is the major critic of San Juan's poetry, and it is
he who has brought out most clearly one important aspect of its
origins (*12*, pp. 219–68). The *Cántico espiritual* is based closely on
the Biblical *Song of Songs,* or *Song of Solomon,* a love poem which
already by the time of its inclusion in the Old Testament was being
interpreted in terms of the love between God and man. A note to
the commentary on the *Llama de amor viva* states that the unusual
metre of this poem was copied from Sebastián de Córdoba's version
a lo divino (that is, a re-writing with a religious meaning) of the
poems of Boscán and Garcilaso; and other borrowings from this
source are not hard to trace. San Juan was therefore familiar with
the *divinización* of secular love poetry, and it is not surprising to find
him applying the same process himself. There are a few direct echoes
of Garcilaso without the intermediary of Córdoba; the glosses are
mostly written round existing *estribillos* which had previously formed
the basis for love songs; and most striking of all, the original of the
Pastorcico has been discovered by José Manuel Blecua in a pastoral
poem which, with only a handful of modifications, San Juan has
converted into a completely acceptable religious lyric.[1]   Dámaso

---

[1]José Manuel Blecua, 'Los antecedentes del poema del *Pastorcico* de San Juan
de la Cruz', *Revista de Filología Española,* XXXIII (1949), 378–80; reprinted
in José Manuel Blecua, *Sobre poesía de la Edad de Oro* (Madrid, Gredos, 1970),
pp. 96–9.

Alonso concludes, therefore, that the Saint's poetry has only two main sources, the *Song of Songs* and secular love poetry; and that in one way or another the whole of his poetic work is the result of a process of *divinización*.

Emilio Orozco has later carried these observations further, revealing a whole tradition of poetry and song *a lo divino* in Franciscan and Carmelite communities, and also another important source for San Juan in the verse of the Italian Franciscan Jacopone da Todi (c. 1236–1306). A Spanish translation of this was published in Lisbon in 1576; and as far as is known San Juan's first poems were written during his imprisonment in the following year (*15*, pp. 115 ff.). Sebastián de Córdoba's *Obras de Boscán y Garcilaso trasladadas a materias cristianas y religiosas* also dates from just about this same time, and there can be little doubt that its appearance in 1575, or else its second edition in 1577, was one of the stimuli that set San Juan on his poetic course.

The question inevitably arises, if so much of the Saint's verse is *divinización,* the refashioning of earlier material in a religious sense, is it any more meritorious than that of Córdoba?   At the end of a whole book on *poesía a lo divino* Professor Bruce W. Wardropper finds himself unable to rate the genre highly: "Ahí está la ironía de la divinización: queriendo ensalzar la poesía y la religión sólo consiguen los poetas a lo divino rebajar una y otra."[2] He makes a distinction, however, between the vulgarizing "contrafacistas" he has been studying and, precisely, the work of San Juan de la Cruz: "San Juan de la Cruz explora los símbolos de su mundo pastoril a lo divino; dista mucho de exponer una alegoría. El simbolismo, método de las investigaciones teológicas y místicas, permite al que lo maneja con destreza traspasar los límites del misterio; la alegoría, método de la vulgarización espiritual, reduce el misterio a las dimensiones de lo ya conocido, niega el misterio" (p. 326).   On the one hand allegory, the vehicle of teaching, on the other sym-

---

[2]Bruce W. Wardropper, *Historia de la poesía lírica a lo divino en la cristiandad occidental* (Madrid, Revista de Occidente, 1958), p. 327.

For an interesting view of *poesía a lo divino* as a literary fashion rather than a serious didactic procedure, see John Crosbie, 'Amoral *a lo divino* poetry in the Golden Age', *Modern Language Review,* LXVI (1971), 599–607.

bolism, the language of the poet; or to put it differently, on the one hand public poetry, on the other hand private. The *Pastorcico* and some of the *Romances* are the only poems of San Juan that can be called allegorical. Elsewhere his borrowings are not the translation into religious terms, for edificatory purposes, of the poetic intuitions of others, but the revivifying of images and conceits through a genuinely fresh intuition; an intuition which finds in them the symbols through which to transmit something of a mystical awareness otherwise defying expression.

II *Mysticism*

Since San Juan's mystical experiences form the subject matter of his finest and most characteristic poems, some examination of the phenomenon of mysticism may help towards their understanding. The first part of this survey owes a great deal to F. C. Happold's *Mysticism* (*20*), an anthology preceded by a very clear and wide-ranging study.

The normal channels through which man apprehends reality are his five senses. On the evidence mediated by the senses he brings his mind to bear, attaining through observation and reason an astonishingly rich awareness of the complex world in which he lives. But the mystic experiences an altogether different kind of awareness, one not mediated through the senses but *im*mediate. Happold defines it as "a development and extension of rational consciousness, resulting in an enlargement and refining of perception, and consequently having a noetic quality, so that through it knowledge of the 'real' is gained which could not be gained through rational consciousness" (*20*, p. 17).

The word derives from the Greek mystery religions, a main feature of which were the initiation rites whereby the adherent was admitted to a secret, inner knowledge of the divine. Mystical awareness has thus always had a numinous quality about it. It is not the prerogative of any one religion: there have been mystics of many faiths, and of none; but it "has its fount in what is the raw material of all religion, and is also the inspiration of much of philosophy, poetry, art, and music, a consciousness of a *beyond,* of something which, though it is interwoven with it, is not of the external world of material phenomena, of an *unseen* over and above the seen" (*20*, pp. 18, 19).

What is the nature of this unique experience which the mystics share? Over many centuries and emanating from widely different countries and religious traditions, their testimonies still agree to a remarkable extent. There is, it seems, an awareness of a new identity, a realization that the old everyday ego is not the true self. The real self exists outside time and space; and to it is afforded an insight into depths of truth that normal consciousness cannot reach.

It perceives intuitively all that is; it is conscious of 'knowing', more completely and certainly than anything has been known before. The senses are found to have been poor transmitters, only a weak, hesitant signal has hitherto been received; but now the soul is freed from dependence on these physical channels. In Blake's phrase the doors of perception are cleansed, and everything appears as it is, infinite.

But it is not an intellectual, objective knowing. "This knowledge is acquired not by way of observation, but by way of participation. The subject does not stand over against the object; the two merge and unite. The knower and the known are one" (*20*, p. 84). The real self therefore both knows and itself partakes of the very essence of reality. The mystic with a religious belief experiences this reality as God. He is not merely in the actual presence of God, he is himself a part of the Godhead, and God of him. This is the mystic union, a complete interpenetration of being. Nor is the union an exclusive one, since all reality is embraced within it. All differentiations cease, and there is a unifying vision of the oneness of everything. "All creaturely existence is experienced as a unity, as All in One and One in All. In theistic mysticism God is felt to be in everything and everything to exist in God" (*20*, p. 46).

The experience is an ecstatic one, intensely pleasurable since the bond of the union, the fabric of the one reality, is apprehended as pure love. Love is seen as Dante saw it, as the principle underlying the whole universe, the force that moves the sun and the other stars. There is no moral dimension here, no sense of a duty to love; love *is*, and whatever is, is love.

Finally, the mystic's awareness comes to him with irresistible authority. "Though he may not be able to describe it in words, though he may not be able logically to demonstrate its validity, to the mystic his experience is fully and absolutely valid and is surrounded with complete certainty" (*20*, p. 19). There is no question of 'belief' in it; he 'knows'.

The description in words is something most mystics have found difficult, because their vision transcended the limits of ordinary rational language. Pascal could only record his two-hour ecstasy in exclamations: "Joy! joy! joy! tears of joy! " San Juan refers repeatedly in his commentaries to the impossibility of the task he has been set: "Por haberse, pues, estas canciones compuesto en amor de abundante inteligencia mística, no se podrán declarar al justo" (Prologue to *Cántico*).[3] "En aquel aspirar de Dios, yo no querría hablar ni aun quiero; porque veo claro que no lo tengo de saber decir" (Final paragraph of *Llama,* first version; *1,* p. 1095). One of the states most difficult to describe is that of complete intuitive knowledge so often attained only through a closing of the eyes to external reality, a shedding of the partial knowledge transmitted through the senses. The mystic feels himself to be knowing and not knowing at the same time. In a work significantly entitled *De docta ignorantia* the fifteenth-century Nicholas de Cusa says: "I was led in the learning that is ignorance to grasp the incomprehensible" (quoted in *20,* p. 42). This language of paradox is one to which many mystics resort in the attempt to convey their experiences. Paradox is already the mode of much New Testament teaching: "He that findeth his life shall lose it, and he that loseth his life for my sake shall find it" (Matthew X, 39); "as sorrowful yet alway rejoicing, as poor yet making many rich, as having nothing and yet possessing all things" (2 Corinthians VI, 10); and the Christian mystics make it their own with their repeated equation of ignorance and knowledge, darkness and day, death and life.

The mystic's other great vehicle of expression is the symbol. The difference between this and the allegory of the poets *a lo divino* has already been referred to, and a similar distinction can be made between the analogy, used for teaching purposes, and the true symbol. When he is drawing on his own experiences for spiritual direction the mystic, like any teacher, will illustrate and clarify by means of apt analogies. Thus Santa Teresa, describing in Chapter 11 of her *Vida* the four stages in the soul's experience of God, likens them to four ways of watering a garden: by drawing water from a well, which is hard work; by the slightly less laborious use of a *noria*; from streams and rivers which only need to be channelled; and best of all through rain, which comes down God-given without any effort on the

[3] *Vida y obras de San Juan de la Cruz.* Biography by P. Crisógono de Jesús, revised by P. Matías del Niño Jesús. Edition of Works by P. Lucinio del SS. Sacramento. (Biblioteca de Autores Cristianos, 4th ed., Madrid, 1960) p. 736. As with the poems, all references to San Juan's commentaries will be to this edition, henceforward referred to by its number in the Bibliography *(1)* .

gardener's part. San Juan similarly illustrates the stages of spiritual progress, in Chapter 10 of the *Noche oscura* commentary, through the image of the log thrown on to a fire, which bit by bit loses its blackness and impurity, and finally becomes inflamed and one with the fire itself. These are both good illustrations that do their job well, and they produce passages of fine prose. But when San Juan in his poetry writes of God as the fountain or the flame; when Dante sees paradise as an unfolding rose, or Emily Brontë welcomes the wind as a powerful, intense spirit of life, these are no longer analogies, but the actual forms in which the experiences came. Nor could they be recorded in any other way at the time, since the symbol is of the essence of the experience. In Baruzi's phrase, the true symbol adheres directly to the experience; it is not the *figure* of an experience (*4*, p. 328).

The mystic's symbolism arises naturally from his apprehension of the oneness of everything, the sense that All is in all. But symbols are of course available to others too, and their role in the collective unconscious of man has been closely studied by C. G. Jung.[4] Only recently has it been fully realized what a density of meaning they give to much medieval and Renaissance art, both literary and representational. J. E. Cirlot in his *Dictionary of Symbols* shows how a great many objects were accepted, at a conscious level, as having a symbolic meaning, and were regularly used pictorially in a kind of iconographic shorthand; but he adds that "in lyrical poetry, alongside works created within the canons of explicit symbolism... there are frequent flowerings of symbolic motifs springing spontaneously out of the creative spirit".[5] It is striking that of the nouns listed by Cirlot at least fifty occur in the handful of San Juan's mystical poems. This is not to say that they are all used with a symbolic content, still less as the inevitable, 'experienced' kind of symbol described above. It does suggest, however, that his poems should be read with some awareness of the levels of meaning that his vocabulary must have carried in the sixteenth century. Their symbolism has recently been examined by Georges Morel (*9*, Vol. III), and the

[4]See particularly C. G. Jung et al., *Man and his Symbols* (London, 1964).
[5]J. E. Cirlot, *A Dictionary of Symbols,* translated by Jack Sage (London, 1962), pp. xxiii–xxiv.

present study will also pay attention to this aspect.

It has been seen how both Santa Teresa and San Juan distinguish successive stages in the soul's progress towards that complete mystical union in which the ground is at last saturated by the rain, and the log incandescent in the fire. Mysticism is not necessarily a continuing and developing process of this kind, and it is not rare to come across people, even among one's own acquaintance, who have had isolated moments of mystical vision, usually quite unexpected and unsought. Pascal has already been mentioned; T. S. Eliot, in *The Dry Salvages,* the third of his *Four Quartets,* describes transitory experiences of this kind:

> For most of us, there is only the unattended
> Moment, the moment in and out of time,
> The distraction fit, lost in a shaft of sunlight,
> The wild thyme unseen, or the winter lightning
> Or the waterfall, or music heard so deeply
> That it is not heard at all, but you are the music
> While the music lasts.

But the title of mystic is generally reserved for those for whom the experiences have become so frequent and normal as almost to constitute a way of life. They have often been members of religious orders, or otherwise free to devote long hours to contemplation, so that their mysticism is in some measure induced; and the pattern of their progress is often the same.

It begins with withdrawal from the world, a purging from all the distractions of the senses, in the so-called 'via purgativa'; this is rewarded with the first intimations of the beyond in the 'via illuminativa', which in turn leads to the complete and lasting union of the 'via unitiva'. The experience of union in the bond of love makes the symbol of marriage a very natural one for many mystics to use, and the second and third stages of the 'mystic way' are sometimes spoken of as betrothal and marriage. But the progress is not always as steady as this. There sometimes intervenes between the early raptures and the final consummation a terrible period of desertion, when the soul has lost contact with God and tries in vain to experience him again. San Juan knew this sense of loss, and called it the dark night of the soul; so that for him the 'way' has a fourfold division: 'la noche del sentido', 'el desposorio espiritual', 'la noche oscura del alma', and 'el matrimonio espiritual'.

The marriage differs in various ways from the betrothal. It is no longer commonly accompanied by trances or violent physical sensations; it is lasting, so that even going about his everyday business the mystic always feels himself to be in the presence of God, and no longer yearns to be liberated from the body by death; and instead of absorbing him utterly, it releases energies which can then be used for the benefit of others. "In the fourth degree the soul goes forth on God's behalf and descends below herself" (Richard of St Victor, quoted in *20,* p. 101). Only at this point, therefore, do the mystic's experiences impinge on the lives of others; only in this ultimate stage does any moral element enter into the phenomenon of mysticism.

It has already been seen that mysticism is not the prerogative of any one faith, and certainly not of Christianity, which William Temple once described as the most avowedly materialist of all the great religions. The more passive, contemplative religions of the east seem in general more attuned to it; and C. Morón Arroyo presents, among other early examples, extracts from three Islamic mystics whose writings show some affinity with those of San Juan (though any direct influence is extremely doubtful).[6] Though the contemplative tradition has always flourished in the Christian church, particularly in Catholicism, it has been in constant tension with the other imperative, the call to good works. The fact that until its culminating stages the mystic way is the way of Mary, to the virtual exclusion of Martha, is no doubt one reason why the Church has sometimes regarded it with suspicion. Another is that if the mystic is able to achieve direct communion with God, he is to some extent obviating the need for the Church and undermining the authority it claims as the mediator of God to man. This consideration was particularly important in the Counter-Reformation period, when the Church was resisting attack, and explains why the writings of Santa Teresa and San Juan did not always find favour with their superiors. The mystic comes too close to two near-heresies, Quietism which turns its back

[6]C. Morón Arroyo, *La mística española. I. Antecedentes y Edad Media* (Madrid, 1971).

on the world and Illuminism which exalts the inner light over
objective ecclesiastical authority, to be allowed complete freedom of
expression.

Far from being necessarily Christian, then, mysticism has at times
seemed to be almost at variance with some aspects of Christianity.
Another point of divergence is that the way in which the mystic
apprehends God often seems to owe relatively little to any exclu-
sively Christian revelation in the person of Jesus, and it is not un-
common for the great contemplatives to describe their insights in
entirely non-scriptural and non-doctrinal terms. With the partial
exception of *La fonte que mana y corre,* there is nothing specifically
Christian in any of San Juan's mystical poems.

A number of literary figures have left records of actual mystical
experience — Dante, Pascal, Blake, Emily Brontë and Eliot have
already been mentioned, and Wordsworth and Shelley also come to
mind — but there is a sense in which all artistic creation has at least
affinities with it. The artist, like the mystic, has powers of perception beyond the normal. He does not so much create, as reach
out to a hidden reality already there, possess it and record it in his
own medium. And it is not even necessary to be such a man apart as
the artist is to attain some forms of consciousness apparently related
to the mystic vision. The modern practice of transcendental meditation seems to be a kind of poor man's mysticism, and to produce
comparable effects: "The bodily after-effects of transcendental meditation include a sense of well-being and an increased ability to cope
with the stress of life. The Christian bystander is reminded of saints
like St Teresa of Avila, who combined prolonged ecstasy with a
relentless energy to the benefit of her Church."[7] The powers of
psychedelic drugs are also well known, and here the evidence of
Aldous Huxley in *The Doors of Perception* (London, 1957) is particularly interesting. He records his sensations after a dose of mescalin,
in language very like that of the mystics: "I was now a Not-self,
simultaneously perceiving and being the Not-self of the things around
me" (p. 27). "In the final stages of egolessness there is an 'obscure
knowledge' that All is in all — that All is actually each" (p. 19). He

[7]Una Kroll, 'Dangers of Transcendental Meditation', in *The Times,* 30th June,
1973.

admits, however, that drugs will not carry one on to the ultimate outgoing phase of humanitarian activity: "In its fullness the way of Mary includes the way of Martha and raises it, so to speak, to its own higher power. Mescalin opens up the way of Mary, but shuts the door on that of Martha" (p. 32). Only among genuine mystics is found "the active-contemplative, the saint, the man who, in Eckhart's phrase, is ready to come down from the seventh heaven in order to bring a cup of water to his sick brother" (p. 32).

The fact that such quasi-mystical states can be made available to ordinary people who have, as far as is known, no unusual spiritual endowment, may be thought by some to invalidate the experiences of San Juan, by others to confirm them. What does seem certain is that an age like the present which is so attracted by extra-sensory perception in its various forms will find a great deal to interest it in the poems of San Juan de la Cruz.

III *Minor Non-mystical Poems*

Romances

The *romances viejos,* or traditional ballads, flourished in Spain in the fifteenth century. They were composed in a fixed metre of octo-syllables with assonance in alternate lines, and are short simple poems by unknown poets directed to an unlearned audience. They were publicly recited or sung, providing entertainment or disseminating news of recent events. This latter function was fulfilled particularly by the *romances fronterizos* which reported the guerrilla fighting between Christians and Moors, in the same way as the contemporary Border Ballads of northern Britain were describing similar skirmishes along another frontier. In either case the ballad was usually a narrative poem, and the poet told his story objectively, in a terse direct style; sometimes highlighting dramatic incidents or elaborating dialogue for the sake of immediacy, but avoiding long descriptions or lyrical digressions, and keeping himself completely out of the picture.

The writing of ballads virtually ceased after 1500, until towards the end of the century the form was revived by Lope de Vega, Góngora and others, but as the vehicle for poetry of a very different kind. The *romances cultos* of these poets are personal and sometimes even autobiographical poems, in their authors' distinctive styles; they often modify the strict ballad metre; and they use all the conscious literary resources of mythology, Petrarchism and stylization which had characterized the Italianate lyric poetry cultivated since the Renaissance. This is no longer popular balladry, but polished writing for a clever and refined readership. But the old ballads had their readers too, as is shown by their inclusion in anthologies and the publication of a whole *Cancionero de romances* in the middle of the sixteenth century. They were still recited, and had also acquired a literary status; so that though they were no longer being written the genre remained as familiar as ever.

The *romance* form must therefore have been a fairly natural choice for San Juan when he had a story to tell. His sequence of nine short ballads on the Creation and the Incarnation may well have been devised originally as an exercise to occupy his mind in his foul

Toledan prison; but it was recited to an audience, as has been seen, at the earliest possible opportunity, and clearly belongs to the tradition of convent verse, to whose combined purposes of instruction and diversion the genre of the *romance viejo* was well suited.

The series begins with a paraphrase of the opening of St John's Gospel, and goes on to describe the Trinity as a union in the bond of love. In *Romances* 2 and 3 the Father proposes to give the Son a wife who will share in the love of the Godhead; and No. 4 depicts the Creation allegorically as the installation of the bride in the lower storey of a rich palace where she will await the coming of the Bridegroom. The allegory lapses in No. 5 where the Jews voice their longing for the coming of Christ, a longing concentrated in No. 6, as the Advent approaches, in the person of old Simeon; but reappears in No. 7 as the Son prepares to meet his bride. The last two pieces recount the Annunciation and the Nativity, the latter being described more as a marriage than as a birth.

The marriage allegory emphasizes the theme of the sequence, which is love. The opening poem is dominated by the word "amor" and its derivatives, sometimes combined in the language of mysticism:

> Tres personas y un amado
> entre todos tres había;
> y un amor en todas ellas,
> y un amante las hacía;
> y el amante es el amado
> en que cada cual vivía.

Their love unites the members of the Trinity in

> un inefable nudo
> que decir no se sabía.

The act of creation is seen as an overflowing of this divine love, and when Christ is born,

> así como desposado
> de su tálamo salía,
> abrazado con su esposa,
> que en sus brazos le traía.[8]

---

[8] The MSS here have "la traía", but "le" makes rather better sense.

But these pieces are very different from San Juan's true mystical poems in which he describes his own intimate experience of God. They are poetically disappointing; and one reason for their lack of success must be the incompatibility of subject matter with form. The *romance* was a narrative genre, and San Juan has a story to tell, but he chooses to tell it largely in terms of abstractions. The Christmas story alone would have provided him with plenty of dramatic incident, of the kind that the *romances viejos* knew how to exploit, had he wished to make use of it; but he is never, in any of his writings, interested in factual detail for its own sake. His purposes of spiritual instruction also required more than a mere relation of well-known events. The unfortunate result is the clothing of relatively subtle thought in an outworn guise, whose archaism is made more jarringly apparent by its unsuitability. Conscious primitivism can be pleasing if well handled, and there are moments like the homely conversation over marriage plans, when God the Son answers his Father's offer of a bride with a "Mucho le agradezco, Padre", which justify Dámaso Alonso's attribution to these poems of an "agraz encanto" (*11*, p. 105). But too often the writing is simplistic rather than simple, and the plodding use of imperfect and conditional verbs to sustain the assonance in -*ía,* though a common device in the old ballads, here has less of medieval quaintness about it than of tiresome jingle.

However much he felt himself bound by the old and much loved genre which he and his prospective hearers knew so well, it remains surprising that a man who at the self-same time was revealing himself as a major poet in the *Cántico espiritual* should not have here found the means to adapt his form and style to a more abstract content. Within ten years' time Lope would have transformed the ballad, with the sometimes violent, sometimes stylized poetic record of his first love affair; but San Juan's *romances* come, formally speaking, at the end of a line, and show very little sign of the imminent renewal.

There is one moment at which the sequence does come to life, and that is in *Romance 5* where words of longing for the Messiah are put into the mouths of the waiting Jews. The content at this point is factual, not figurative, and the manner of the traditional *romances* is not inappropriate. In particular their common device of direct speech to gain immediacy and eliminate distance is here used to good effect.

Some speakers wish that the coming might be in their time, and that they might see and touch God. Others demand, with urgent imperatives,

> Acaba, Señor;
> al que has de enviar, envía,

or

> Regad, nubes de lo alto,
> que la tierra lo pedía,
> y ábrase ya la tierra,
> que espinas nos producía,
> y produzca aquella flor
> con que ella florecería.

The likening of God to life-giving water is a very natural metaphor, particularly for dwellers in dry countries, and one found frequently in the Bible. Here San Juan is almost certainly recalling Psalm 72: "He shall come down like rain upon the mown grass; as showers that water the earth" (v.6). But his word "espinas" also echoes a more recent source: in Garcilaso's surroundings too the presence or absence of a loved one had made the difference between flowers and thorns. Pointing the contrast for the ear as well as for the eye, by a clever variation of pace and rhythm which San Juan's metric regularity denies him, he tells how after Elisa's death

> La tierra, que de buena
> gana nos producía
> flores con que solía
> quitar en sólo vellas mil enojos,
> produce agora en cambio estos abrojos,
> ya de rigor de espinas intratable.

> > (*Egloga* I, lines 302–7)

The most striking moment in San Juan's ballad sequence is thus one in which popular, biblical and Renaissance influences are combined, in a manner which will be seen to be characteristic of his finest writing.

The last *romance* of the series, though it lacks the vigour of No. 5, is of more interest than the others in that it alone makes the attempt to match relative sophistication of thought with an appropriate style. It has already been seen that this short poem gives a twist to the story of the Nativity by presenting it as at the same time a birth and

a marriage, the union of God with humanity. Jesus leaving his
mother's womb is a bridegroom coming forth out of his chamber
(a reminiscence of Psalm 19); he takes his bride in his arms as his
mother rocks him in hers. This is an excellent example of a *concepto,*
or conceit; a clever idea which unites normally unrelated elements in
such a way as to bring out a greater density of meaning. *Conceptismo*
was to be a characteristic of much seventeenth-century writing,
particularly in the works of Góngora and Quevedo; but in San Juan's
time the vogue for it was only just beginning, and this is one of the
very few instances found in his poems. He carries his *concepto*
further with a pleasing image: the angels sing in the heavens,

> festejando el desposorio
> que entre tales dos había.
> Pero Dios en el pesebre
> allí lloraba y gemía;
> que eran joyas que la esposa
> al desposorio traía.

Tears which are like pearls are a commonplace of Italianate verse, but
here the context, making these pearls into bridal jewels, gives the
trite metaphor a richer meaning. This *romance* heralds the *artificio*
of better-known Christmas poems like those of Lope's *Pastores de
Belén* (1612) or Góngora's "Caído se le ha un clavel" (1621), and
unlike its eight predecessors does at last begin to point the way
forward.

One final *romance,* not belonging to the series, paraphrases Psalm
137, "By the waters of Babylon we sat down and wept, when we
remembered thee, O Zion". Although it elaborates its original,
making the singer voice his longing for his native land in the language
of love, it cannot be said to improve upon it. There is a skilful bit of
divinización in the last verse, where, faced with the psalmist's astonishing imprecation, "O daughter of Babylon . . . happy shall he be
that taketh and dasheth thy little ones against the stones", San Juan
renders these stones as "la piedra que era Cristo", to whom the little
children are to be united. The only other passage of some slight
interest is the quatrain

> Yo me metía en su fuego,
> sabiendo que me abrasaba,

desculpando al avecica
que en el fuego se acababa,

in which the singer bewails the hopelessness of his longing for Zion.
What is this "avecica"? María Rosa Lida takes it to be the mythical
phoenix which burns itself to death and rises again from its own ashes
(*14*, p. 45, note 1); but it would seem to be more probably the
butterfly − admittedly not a bird, but a creature who, because of
its fatal attraction to the candle flame, had served poets from Petrarch
onwards as a figure of the unwise lover who knows his love will
destroy him but cannot give it up. In either case the allusion is a
culto one, and illustrates again San Juan's fusion of biblical with
Renaissance material.

Pastorcico'

If the *Romances* have received at best a lukewarm response from
critics, the *Pastorcico* has, in the words of one of them, been singled
out for special affection (*6*, p. 95). Dámaso Alonso, writing in
1942, noted that it lacked the force, the luminescence, the intox-
ication of the mystical poems, and that it made no use of imagery,
but praised its simplicity, its tenderness and delicate atmosphere (*11*,
p.55). Blecua (see p.13, n.1, above) calls it an "encantador poemita".

Blecua's discovery in 1949, in a MS. of the Bibliothèque Nationale,
Paris, of the poem from which it clearly derives, made plain for the
first time how much of the *Pastorcico* was borrowed. Dámaso Alonso
had already conjectured that it was a work of *divinización,* a re-
casting of a pastoral original which might one day come to light,
and this proved to be the case. The source poem is as follows:

Un pastorcillo solo está penado,
ajeno de placer y de contento,
y en su pastora firme el pensamiento,
y el pecho del amor muy lastimado.

No llora por pensar que está olvidado,
que ningún miedo tiene del olvido,
mas porque el corazón tiene rendido,
y el pecho del amor muy lastimado.

> Mas dice el pastorcico: ¡Desdichado!
> ¿qué haré cuando venga el mal de ausencia,
> pues tengo el corazón en la presencia
> y el pecho del amor muy lastimado?
>
> Imagínase ya estar apartado
> de su bella pastora en tierra ajena,
> y quédase tendido en el arena,
> y el pecho del amor muy lastimado.

The unusual metre (a hybrid in which the a b b a rhyme-scheme of the old octosyllabic *redondilla* is imposed on Italianate hendeca-syllables), the refrain, the vocabulary and many of the actual lines are already there. So is the figure of the suffering shepherd, which almost cries out to be treated *a lo divino* as Sebastián de Córdoba had done with the shepherds of Garcilaso. Córdoba in fact provided the means for the transformation, for, as Dámaso Alonso had already shown, the lovesick shepherd's death on a tree in San Juan's final stanza has its origin in Córdoba's version of Garcilaso's Second Eclogue (*11,* pp. 58–9). San Juan had merely to add this stanza, the only one with no antecedent in the source poem, and change the main cause of grief from impending absence to unrequited love, to turn the pastoral lyric into an allegory of the Crucifixion.

Re-examining the *Pastorcico* in 1962 in the light of Blecua's discovery, Dámaso Alonso marvels at the skill of the adaptation, carried through so smoothly that no join is apparent. He notes that San Juan does not use the refrain in his second stanza, a sign of his relative indifference to formal regularity; and he comments, as any critic must, on the superiority of the re-working over its insipid original (*12,* pp. 245–7 and 271–3).

He like Blecua assumes without hesitation that it is San Juan's poem which is the derivative, and not the other way round; but two critics have in fact queried this order of priority. P. Emeterio Setién de Jesús María, examining the whole question of San Juan's sources in *Las raíces de la poesía sanjuanista y Dámaso Alonso* (Burgos, 1950), argues that the *Pastorcico* might well be the earlier work, and that if it were not it could hardly rank as one of San Juan's poems, adhering as closely as it does to the secular version. This is to ignore the refining and re-fashioning that has clearly taken place, despite the extent of the borrowings; moreover P. Emeterio's truculent tone and unwillingness to admit to a secular source for any of the Saint's writings make of him a far from reliable critic. Max Milner's approach in *Poésie et vie mystique chez Saint Jean de la Croix* (Paris, 1951), is much cooler, though his argument seems unsound. He maintains that if San Juan had indeed based the *Pastorcico* on the poem discovered by Blecua, it would follow that he must have transformed, through no more than changes of detail and a veneer of religious symbolism, a thoroughly insipid piece of amorous verse into a pure jewel of mystic love (*8*, p. 129). Stated in these terms the achievement might have been unlikely, but I see the *Pastorcico* as something less than a pure jewel of mystic love. A smooth, skilful and appealing poem it undoubtedly is, and to create such a work out of an inferior original by means of a few deft touches is certainly not beyond the power of a master. There can be no serious reason for doubting that San Juan knew the secular poem and re-wrote it *a lo divino,* particularly as it bears the heading "Otras canciones a lo divino" in the Sanlúcar MS.

We have, then, a poem which is a close re-working of a pastoral lyric, with an additional stanza based on Sebastián de Córdoba's identification of the Arcadian shepherd with Christ. This final twist converts the whole poem into a religious work, an allegory of the Crucifixion. But though the ending may be unexpected there is no disjointedness to impair the unity of the poem. Its most notable formal characteristic is its smooth, unhurried rhythm. The flow of this poem compared with the lameness of many lines in the original provides ample evidence of San Juan's mastery of the hendecasyllable.

Like the *Romances* it describes the actions of Christ in largely abstract language. The only concrete terms, apart from those pertaining to the pastoral convention − "pastor", "pastora", "pecho", "corazón" − are "tierra ajena", "árbol" and "brazos". We have here a stylized Crucifixion, as in *Romance* 9 we have a stylized Nativity. And here perhaps the limitations of the poem begin to be apparent. Stylization and allegory are legitimate literary procedures, but they do not carry the force and authority of that symbolism which is felt to be the only possible expression of a deep personal experience. The allegory is not even technically perfect, since in terms of the surface story why should a slighted shepherd climb up into a tree to die?

The shepherd of the source poem throwing himself down on the sand in his despair is a more credible figure. San Juan's version only makes real sense if the underlying meaning is invoked, but allegory should succeed at both levels.

Not only is he using borrowed words and a borrowed metaphor: the emotion of the poem too seems second-hand, or at least less intimately felt than that of his greater works. The love it describes is not, as Milner states, mystical; it is not the blazing, overwhelming apprehension of total reality as love which San Juan elsewhere expresses through such compelling symbols; and the *Pastorcico* therefore lacks both the imaginative richness and the transcendence of his three poetic masterpieces. It is not insincere, but it has about it perhaps a little too much of the devotional as well as the poetic exercise, and its tone becomes rather too mellifluous. It makes a strong initial appeal, but in my experience at least does not retain it, and soon begins to cloy.

Gicovate rightly classes the *Pastorcico* among the "diversions of a great mind" (6, p. 95). It is much more successful than the *Romances*. A good pianist can create beautiful sounds when practising arpeggios, and San Juan has here written a poem of great charm, particularly attractive to the ear. It is indeed an "encantador poemita"; but it is difficult to see it as anything more.

La fonte que mana y corre

It may seem questionable at first whether *La fonte* should be included among San Juan's minor poems, since it opens so magnificently. Here is a poem which is boldly and triumphantly personal: " ¡Que bien sé yo! "; and which immediately finds expression for the certainty it proclaims in the two great symbols of the fountain and the night. The pity is that it ends so drably.

Although in his edition of the *Poesías completas* Dámaso Alonso prints the opening phrase in two lines, as is customary, he believes it to have been originally a three-line stanza, with an assonance in $o - e$ which explains the use of the form "fonte" rather than the normal diphthongized "fuente":

> Que bien sé yo la fonte
> que mana y corre,
> aunque es de noche.

Such a stanza, with its typical introductory "que" (not in this case exclamatory), has all the flavour of popular medieval verse, and is in all probability a traditional *estribillo* (see p. 37), which San Juan proceeds to gloss: another instance of *divinización*. If this is so the poem is, like the *Pastorcico*, hybrid in form, since an old Spanish verse is glossed in couplets of Italianate hendecasyllables, the last line of the verse recurring each time as a refrain (*12*, pp. 276–7).

If the *estribillo* is borrowed, it offers San Juan the very elements he needs for the expression of his mystical awareness. Water is, as always, a principle of life, and here it is specifically a fountain which springs and flows, an abundant vital source. The poet knows it, intimately and personally – the first person is doubly emphasized, with verb and pronoun – and with complete certainty, even in darkness. The "noche" here may well have meant for San Juan the gloom of his prison cell, in which ecstasy could still be attained; but it also represents the peculiar quality of mystic 'knowing', a knowledge which is independent of external stimuli. The fountain

is hidden, inwardly known.   Cirlot in his *Dictionary of Symbols*
defines the fountain as the mystical centre, the source of power and
life in the depths of all being; it can therefore only be sought out in
secrecy and darkness.

But the stanzas which follow, after the first one, dwell rather on
the limitless immensity of the flowing stream: it cannot be forded,
or its depths plumbed; it waters heaven and earth and all mankind.
And yet the obsessive darkness is always there in the refrain. The
poem is thus based on a typically mystical paradox: the hidden and
secretly known which is at the same time universal and transcendent.
There is a double movement, an inward penetration and an outward
expansiveness, pivoting each time on the word "aunque".

The climax of the poem comes at the point where the night is
precisely contrasted with "claridad" and "toda luz", and the paradox
becomes complete. It was this stanza which moved a much more
recent poet, Pedro Salinas, to write: "There is created, by a kind of
poetic miracle, a sensation of darkness which instead of being negat-
ive, of preventing one from seeing, is positive, helps one to see, and
does not obliterate the seeing of the soul, the marvelous inner vision.
It is the revelation of light through darkness."[9]

Thereafter the poem declines. The verse becomes pedestrian, and
the symbolism of the fountain first dwindles into a lame allegory of
the formation of the Trinity, and is then uneasily linked with the
idea of God's presence in the Sacrament. The quality of mystic
knowing is again made apparent here, but this time by contrast. San
Juan laments in another gloss his inability to experience God fully in
Communion, and here it is very plain that though he can 'see' him in
the Host with the eye of belief — "en este pan de vida yo la *veo*" —
it is as the free-flowing river in the unseeing darkness that he 'knows'
him.[10]

Glosses

The other five poems in which San Juan glosses a three or four-line

[9]Pedro Salinas, *Reality and the Poet in Spanish Poetry,* English text by
Edith Fishtine Helman (Baltimore, 1940), p. 125.

[10]A somewhat different exposition of this poem is given by Helmut Hatzfeld,
7, pp. 332–48.

verse form a recognizable group. All are in octosyllables, in stanzas of similar length (seven, eight or nine lines); their structural patterns are identical, or very nearly so; and they all belong to the same well-established poetic genre.

Most popular poetry in medieval Spain took the form either of the *romance* or of the *villancico.* This latter is a poem based on an *estribillo* (a brief verse of two, three or four lines, simple and song-like, usually touching on rustic life or love), the *estribillo* being developed in one or more longer stanzas which constitute the *glosa,* or gloss. (The *estribillo* is itself sometimes known as a *villancico,* but this nomenclature makes for confusion between the initial short stanza and the whole poem.) The *villancico* acquired literary respectability much earlier than the *romance,* and examples are to be found in the *cancioneros* (anthologies) of the later fifteenth century. But already at this early stage they are beginning to undergo development at the hands of courtly poets. It is becoming a common practice to replace a popular *glosa* by a cultured one, or to supply a cultured *glosa* if only the *estribillo* exists. In the next phase of development poets will sometimes gloss courtly *estribillos* of their own composition, in a pastiche of the popular mode. Having thus evolved at a relatively early stage into a form acceptable to cultured poets, the *villancico* escapes the fate of the plebeian *romance,* and continues to flourish uninterruptedly throughout the sixteenth century, alongside the Italianate poetry then also in vogue.

In the middle of that century there appeared the first of a number of *cancioneros* of a more specialized kind, the *Cancionero espiritual* (Valladolid, 1549), which is an anthology of religious poems. And it is not surprising to find that many of these are adaptations of secular *villancicos.* In his re-writing of Boscán and Garcilaso, Sebastián de Córdoba was in fact merely applying to Italianate poetry a process of *divinización* that was already long familiar in the field of the *villancico.* Dámaso Alonso distinguishes three kinds of composition in the *Cancionero espiritual:* those which are entirely original, developing an initial verse of the author's own invention, those which add a new religious gloss to an existing *estribillo,* and those which modify the *estribillo* itself to give it a spiritual meaning. The religious lyric of this type therefore both parallels and extends the secular treatment of the *villancico* in the fifteenth and sixteenth centuries.

It also frequently uses a similar style. The nature of *cancionero* love-poetry has been very well indicated by R. O. Jones (*13*, pp. 29–30). It was a late flowering of the medieval convention of courtly love. The *cancionero* poet voices his sufferings in a language of narrow range but great intensity. His vocabulaιy is small, and he uses little imaginative colour, but achieves his effects rather through rhetorical devices involving word-play. Jones lists three of these: "oxymoron, antithesis, and polyptoton (repetition of a word or forms of a word), all three expressive of the tormented obsession of the lover, helpless in the grip of contradictions, willing his own martyrdom but yearning for release, thrown from extreme to extreme of joy and pain, hope and despair" (*13*, p. 30).

These are not the emotions of San Juan de la Cruz. But antithesis is the common language of the mystic, and he therefore finds a natural mode of expression in the manner of the *cancioneros.* Three of the five *estribillos* glossed by him contain clear paradoxes: "vivo sin vivir", "muero porque no muero", "sin arrimo y con arrimo"; "no sabiendo, toda ciencia trascendiendo"; and the close, insistent probing of these contradictions is as appropriate to his intense spiritual emotion as it was to the anguish of the love poets. San Juan is thus once again in these poems writing wholly within a long-established tradition, that of the *villancico,* which glossed an anonymous or newly composed *estribillo* in a number of octosyllabic stanzas; and more particularly in that branch of the tradition which elaborates the initial verse in a religious sense, often in the concentrated antithetical manner of the love poets of the *cancioneros.*

The verse "Vivo sin vivir en mí" illustrates perfectly this antithetical manner. The paradox of death in life and life in death, which in its union of incompatibles heralds the seventeenth-century *concepto,* was frequently used by *cancionero* poets; Max Milner quotes three examples (*8,* p. 89). It succinctly describes the despair of the hopeless lover, but since "morir" was sometimes a euphemism for sexual release, it could also be read with a titillating ambiguity. The possibility of this more physical but more optimistic meaning perhaps paradoxically made it easier to elaborate in a religious sense, since the spiritual aspirant also hopes positively, for a death which will bring not only an end to longing but a lasting and glorious fulfilment. The fact that the same stanza was also glossed by Santa

Teresa seems to suggest that its interpretation *a lo divino* was already traditional. Its stress on present frustration and future consummation makes it not altogether a suitable vehicle for the mystic, who achieves his union with God in this life; or at least suitable only for those in the earlier stages of the 'mystic way', whose experiences of union are still only transitory and leave deep dissatisfaction in their wake. Santa Teresa partially solves this problem by devoting two stanzas largely to the first line, which she is able to interpret positively, in the sense of a life lived in God:

> Vivo ya fuera de mí,
> después que muero de amor;
> porque vivo en el Señor
> que me quiso para sí.[11]

San Juan's poem is entirely one of yearning, and could hardly be classified as a mystical poem but for one or two hints that he has already known a bliss which he cannot now recapture. "En mí yo no vivo *ya*"; the inadequacy of the Sacrament as a mediator of God; and the fear of loss which is stronger than the hope of attainment, all suggest either that this poem dates from San Juan's passage through the 'dark night of the soul', or that the words of the *estribillo* have led him to recall the emotions of that period.

The latter seems slightly more probable, in that the poem is not particularly compelling and does not seem to have issued from any recent deep experience. There is polyptoton in the obsessive weaving around the words "vivo", "vida", "vivir", but the tension which this device can sometimes generate here declines into the maudlin "Lástima tengo de mí"; and the figure of the fish glad to be taken from the water because it is going to die, far from offering an enriching image, is merely silly. Again we are dealing with a devotional exercise, and not a particularly successful one.[12]

[11]Santa Teresa de Jesús, *Obras completas* (Madrid, Aguilar, 1945), p. 717. This poem seems to be correctly attributed to Santa Teresa. Two other glosses on the same theme which have often appeared under her name are amalgams of some of her stanzas with some of those of San Juan; see the introduction by P. Silverio de Santa Teresa to *Obras de Santa Teresa de Jesús* (Burgos, 1915–24), Vol. VI, pp. lxi–lxiii.

[12]Hatzfeld gives a more favourable exposition of this poem, *7*, pp. 167–209.

There is no doubt at all about the mystical content of "Entréme donde no supe". In the MS. the poem bears the description "Coplas hechas sobre un éxtasis de harta contemplación". The *estribillo* is not known in any other connection and is probably San Juan's own; and it must have been conceived with a mystical meaning from the beginning. It contradicts initially the confident affirmation of "Que bien sé yo la fonte", but only to re-state something like it in the third line, "toda ciencia trascendiendo". Mystic knowing is here described through paradox alone rather than symbol. The 'night' in which the senses cease to convey information has become 'not knowing', and the 'knowledge' of the fountain is here the trans-cendence of all knowledge of the everyday kind. There is the same penetration to a hidden, secret place in the opening word "Entréme", followed in "quedéme" by a prolonged passivity in a state exceeding human awareness.

The first stanza of the gloss reiterates the negatives — "no supe", "sin saber", "no diré", "no sabiendo" — the second stresses the soli-tude and secrecy. A cluster of three adjectives, "embebido", "absorto", "enajenado", then describes the separation from self which leads to a strange new understanding, an "entender no enten-diendo". (One recalls Aldous Huxley's "I was now a Not-self, simul-taneously perceiving and being the Not-self of the things around me".) In the fifth strophe abstractions yield momentarily to symbols. There is first the symbol of flight, expressive of detachment; but it too means absence of knowledge:

> Cuanto más alto se sube
> tanto menos se entendía . . .

This upward soaring is the antithesis of the inner penetration of "Entréme donde no supe", so that as in *La fonte* a dual movement holds the poem in tension. Then the night reappears, a night which again is all brightness, and this time without even an "aunque" to mark the distinction:

> que es la tenebrosa nube
> que a la noche esclarecía.

A reference to Exodus XIV in the margin of the Sanlúcar MS. here makes plain the source of this astonishing image: the pillar of fire by night and cloud by day which guided the Israelites through the desert,

and which ultimately assumed both forms at once, obscuring the
vision of the pursuing Egyptians at the same time as it lit the way
across the Red Sea for the Children of Israel. San Juan was fascin-
ated by this "nubes tenebrosa et illuminans noctem" which accorded
so well with his own experience, and returned to it in one of his
prose commentaries, the *Subida del Monte Carmelo* (II, 3, iv, v; *1,*
p. 455), when he was working out the connotations of the "noche
oscura". There he saw the pillar as a symbol of faith, which darkens
the everyday light of understanding while illuminating in a quite
different manner of its own. In this gloss, however, he is content to
let his image stand without explanation, as the boldest of paradoxes.
After further development of the idea of "saber no sabiendo" he
does round off his poem with an attempt to be more explicit:

> Y si lo queréis oír,
> consiste esta suma ciencia
> en un subido sentir
> de la divinal Esencia;

but this concession to rational thought makes far less impact than
his mystic and poetic symbol of the radiant darkness.

"Tras de un amoroso lance" describes the pursuit of love by means
of the metaphor of falconry. In so doing it follows a long poetic
tradition according to which, in the words of Gil Vicente, "la caza
de amor es de altanería". The heading to San Juan's poem, "Otras a
lo divino", suggests that it was based on a precise secular source
within this tradition, and Dámaso Alonso has discovered this source
poem in a MS. of the Biblioteca Nacional (*12,* p. 243). Its *estribillo*
read:

> Tras de un amoroso lance,
> aunque de esperanzas falto,
> subí tan alto, tan alto,
> que le di a la caza alcance.

This was easily *divinizado* by modifying the second line to allow the
lover some measure of hope; and it provided San Juan not merely
with an evocative if well-worn image, but also with a context for
what has already been seen to be for him a significant symbol, that
of flight. The whole poem this time is full of soaring, conveyed
almost as a physical sensation. Actual levitation does sometimes

accompany ecstatic states — instances were recorded in the case of
Santa Teresa — but even without this external manifestation there
can be little doubt that San Juan is here describing the almost
physical quality that his raptures had for him. Detachment from
reality is experienced as a liberating flight. It needs a moment of
abandonment to let go; San Juan makes a "ciego y oscuro salto", in
just the same way as, years later, Emily Brontë was to write of her
spirit's leap into the void:

> Measuring the gulf it stoops, and dares the final bound.
>
> *(The Complete Poems of Emily Jane Brontë,*
> ed. C. W. Hatfield, New York, 1941, No.190)

Emilio Orozco is the critic who has brought out most fully the
sense of airiness and space in the poetry of San Juan de la Cruz
(*15,* pp. 224–8); and nowhere is this quality more apparent than in
this poem about the hawk on the wing. The bird flies so high that it
loses itself from sight; and even that is not high enough: "mil vuelos
pasé de un vuelo". But Orozco fails to link the spaciousness with the
opposing sense of hidden darkness with which it is often so closely
related; and not merely as a contrast, but as two aspects of the same
thing. In this poem, once again, the light and the darkness seem to
be one: the eye is so dazzled with brightness that the capture takes
place in the dark; the leap of love is "ciego y oscuro", but it carries
the lover up into the light. And the same uncertainty exists between
upward and downward trajectories. The higher the flight, the deeper
the descent into despair of ever reaching the goal; but this "abatir"
of the spirit is also the "abatíme tanto, tanto" which finally captures
the quarry. Is the bird climbing up to its prey, or swooping down
upon it? The violent contradictions of this vertiginous flight suggest
the mystic's ecstasies as no logical language could.

   The remaining glosses are those which do not figure in the Sanlúcar
MS. revised by San Juan, and therefore lack the guarantee of
authenticity; but their appearance in the MS. of Jaén and their close
affinity with the last three poems considered may be thought to
establish their authorship beyond reasonable doubt. "Sin arrimo y
con arrimo" is a true gloss in the strict sense, since its three stanzas
respectively elaborate and end with the three lines of the *estribillo*
in turn. (The other poems of the group all gloss their initial verse in
a more general manner, and the last line only is repeated as a refrain

at the end of every stanza.) The *estribillo* is unknown elsewhere, and may be original. The opening contradiction and the twofold mention of darkness certainly sound like the language of mysticism, though since the last line could equally well have been written by a love poet the possibility of another modification *a lo divino* cannot be excluded. The first strophe dwells on detachment from the world and from self, the second seems at first to refer to actual darkness – the darkness of the Toledan cell? – but then lifts it up into a mystical paradox. The last stanza is a little surprising. In it we encounter for the first time in this study of San Juan's poems, but not the last, the symbol of burning as the means by which self is purged in the mystic transformation into love. Yet suggestive as the word "consumiendo" is in this sense, San Juan takes it up with only one other related word, "llama"; and it is a quite different pair, "sabor" and "sabroso", that from their positions at the end of the fourth and the sixth lines seem to bear much of the weight of the strophe. "Sabroso" is fairly common in sixteenth-century verse meaning simply 'pleasant', 'delightful'; Garcilaso's shepherds sing a "cantar sabroso" (*Egloga* I, line 4). Yet here the juxtaposition with "sabor" reinforces the sense of 'tasty', and makes of "llama sabrosa" an unusually striking paradox: love is a consuming fire, but one that can be relished.

The word "sabor" also opens the first stanza of the final gloss: and here the whole poem is given over to the development of this unexpected metaphor. The *estribillo* speaks of "toda la hermosura", which the poet prizes less than a chance "no sé qué". It was originally, as Dámaso Alonso has shown, the nucleus of a *culto* love poem (*11,* pp. 116–17 and *12,* pp. 239–40); but the inexplicit and inexpressible "no sé qué" can serve San Juan's mystical purpose equally well. What is surprising is the twist he gives it. Beauty is most often thought of as visual, and the source poem is in fact contrasting the looks of the 'dumb blonde' with the greater attractiveness of her more vivacious sister. (Dámaso's interpretation of it as a neoplatonic poem delicately poised between the human and the divine does not seem to me to be borne out by such lines as "un donaire extraordinario/que promete maravillas . . . ".) Yet San Juan develops the idea in terms of the sense of taste. Much of his vocabulary is concerned with eating: "sabor", "apetito", "paladar", "dulzura", "hartura", "manjar"; even in the more abstract second half of the poem the line which concludes each stanza is repeatedly introduced by some form of "gustar". The most striking stanza is the third, where the state of the mystic who has 'lost his taste' for the world is likened to that of a sick man whom fever has robbed of his appetite. This is undoubtedly more of an analogy than an inevitable symbol; and there is a biblical precedent for the metaphor in Psalm 34, verse 8, "Oh taste and see that the Lord is good". But its application and development here are ingenious, and could only be the work of one who had known at first hand that spiritual delirium in which values are transformed.

San Juan's five octosyllabic glosses in the *cancionero* manner vary in quality, both one poem from another and between different stanzas of the same poem. At times they barely rise above the pedestrian level of the *Romances,* elsewhere they succeed in giving such genuine poetic expression to the mystic experience as to suggest that they ought not to be so frequently passed over. Together with the better known *Fonte que mana y corre* (also a gloss on an *estribillo* but in a different metre), they move in the world of mystic symbols, and show at least some measure of affinity with the three masterpieces on which San Juan's fame as a poet chiefly rests.

R. O. Jones has emphasized the striking effects of Renaissance influences on the lyric poetry of Spain. It was not simply a matter of the
old eight-syllable line giving ground to the Italian heptasyllable and
hendecasyllable, marked as the effects of the new rhythms were. A
whole new mood and manner came to dominate:

> The rhetorical and lexical range of the new poetry is far greater
> than that of the old. In love-poetry, Petrarch and the Italian
> Petrarchans being now the dominant influence, Petrarch's charac-
> teristic use of nature as the source of much of his imagery and as
> a back-drop for his self-analysis is imitated by Garcilaso and
> Boscán. This had an immensely liberating effect on the poets'
> imagination: the universe becomes their stage. By contrast, the
> poetry of their predecessors is claustrophobic in atmosphere. The
> new poetry is further enriched by the influence of the major
> Latin poets, above all Virgil and Horace. This vast enlargement of
> the language of poetry permitted deeper and more subtle explora-
> tion of states of mind and conduced to a more sensitive awareness
> of the outside world. The result is a poetry richer in texture and
> colour and so capable of more vivid sensorial effects, and capable
> too of greater conceptual complexity. (*13*, p. 33)

An analogous sense of liberation is felt by the reader who turns
from San Juan's glosses in the *cancionero* manner to his three poems
in *lira* metre. There is no warrant for thinking of a chronological
progression in San Juan's case: it has already been seen that he was
capable of writing very different kinds of poetry at the same time.
Nevertheless it is difficult to escape the feeling of advance as one
passes from the tense concentration of the glosses to poems marked
by expansiveness, by a wide vocabulary and a full range of sense
impressions, and by a rich depiction of the natural background; even
though that background figures symbolically rather than in its own
right.

Tasso's five-line *lira* stanza with its careful arrangement of rhymes
and of long and short lines is a metre of great emotive power.

Garcilaso was the first Spanish poet to use it, in his Fifth *Canción.*
Luis de León had chosen it for many of his poems of contemplation
and spiritual longing, and his example may have influenced San Juan;
though Orozco suggests a perhaps more likely inspiration in the
Spanish translation of the religious lyrics of Jacopone da Todi published at Lisbon in 1576. This volume includes both a poem in strict
lira metre and also one in the six-line *lira* which San Juan was to use
in the *Llama de amor viva.* Both express the anguish of the soul which
has known God and lost him, and it is probable that they made a more
than superficial impression on the Spanish mystic *(15,* 129–33).

Noche oscura

Dámaso Alonso has pointed to two distinct influences on the language
of this poem. Garcilaso had described in his Second Eclogue how a
despairing lover left his house at dead of night:

> La quinta noche, en fin, mi cruda suerte,
> queriéndome llevar do se rompiese
> aquesta tela de la vida fuerte,
>   hizo que de mi choza me saliese
> por el silencio de la noche oscura
> a buscar un lugar donde muriese;

(Egloga II, lines 533–8)

and climbed up a steep hillside to sit in the fresh breeze at the foot of
an elm. In Sebastián de Córdoba's version the parallel is even closer:
the "barranco" has become a "torre", and memory recalls love scenes
that had taken place on that very spot, "entre dos almenas" *(11,*
pp. 44, 70–71). A much earlier love poem, the *Song of Songs,* also
speaks of a going forth at night, this time in search of the beloved:
"By night on my bed I sought him whom my soul loveth; I sought
him but I found him not. I will rise now and go about the city in the
streets, and in the broad ways I will seek him whom my soul loveth"
(III, 1, 2); and later of the loved one feeding "among the lilies"
(VI, 3). Moreover the whole conception of San Juan's poem, a
girl's account of a meeting with her lover, while by no means as
closely modelled on the *Song of Songs* as is the *Cántico espiritual,*
clearly owes something to it. Two earlier poetic traditions are fused

here to produce a new and fully integrated work (*11*, pp. 157–60).

For some critics the essence of this poem is the powerful symbol of the night. Night was an important attendant circumstance in the *Fonte que mana y corre;* here the poet exults in it. Darkness dominates the first three stanzas, with night gradually taking on a more and more positive identity. At first it is simply "oscura", then it becomes "dichosa"; and by the middle of the poem it is "amable", and fully personified as the entity which has actively guided the lovers to their meeting. Night is much more than an indifferent setting, it is the essential catalyst for the union.

San Juan himself makes plain the importance the symbol of night held for him, in his insistence on it in the two commentaries inspired by this poem, the *Subida del Monte Carmelo* and the *Noche oscura.* Neither of these treatises extends beyond the third stanza of the poem, so that the word "noche" is central to them both; and it is really little more than this one word that they expound, detailing the various kinds of purgation that the soul must undergo. The *Noche oscura* commentary distinguishes between the two successive 'nights', the oblivion of the senses and the agonized 'dark night of the soul', and though the poem is not at all concerned with the latter, the commentary describes it in vivid and pungent language: "De tal manera la destrica y decuece la sustancia espiritual, absorbiéndola en una profunda y honda tiniebla, que el alma se siente estar deshaciendo y derritiendo en la haz y vista de sus miserias con muerte de espíritu cruel; así como si, tragada de una bestia, en su vientre tenebroso se sintiese estar digeriéndose, padeciendo estas angustias como Jonás en el vientre de aquella marina bestia' (II, 6, i; *1*, p. 675).

It is not surprising that many exponents of San Juan's work as a whole similarly make much of this symbol. For P. Lucinio, "la idea de la *Noche* es la creación simbolista más original y fecunda de la doctrina del Doctor Místico" (*1*, p. 405). For Baruzi it is an original intuition, and even in a sense the one true symbol dominating his work, other figurative analogies like physical love constituting no more than allegories (*4*, pp. 300–339). Two more recent French critics, Max Milner (*8*, p. 112) and Georges Morel (*9*, Vol. III, pp. 159–74), rectify this obvious exaggeration and also the unwarranted claim of originality, pointing to a number of antecedents, particularly in the Old Testament (as indeed the Saint himself had been at pains to do, with the many biblical references in his prose texts); and Helmut Hatzfeld suggests the possible influences of Ruysbroeck and Ramon Llull (*7*, pp.73–93). All these three scholars, however, stress the remarkable development of the idea in the hands of San Juan, and Morel still sees in his work the particular importance of the symbol of night, which he calls symbol of symbols (p. 159).

Nevertheless if the poem is studied on its own without reference to the incomplete commentaries, then night is seen to be only one, and probably the less important, of the two related symbols out of which it is built. Night is the wonderful mediator who has brought the lovers together; but the purpose of the purgation of the soul is to lead to the experience of God, and the symbol of night leads naturally and necessarily to the symbol of physical love. Baruzi, who is unwilling to see sexual love as more than an analogy or at best a borrowed pseudo-symbol in San Juan's teaching, belittles what he sees as the artificial reminiscences of the last three stanzas of this poem in relation to the pure poetry of the first five; but this is to dichotomize a work which is in fact a perfect unity. The poem has its phases, but they are those of a single experience.

A recent analysis by R. O. Jones makes this plain, and provides a necessary corrective to Baruzi's view (*13*, p. 111). He shows how the poem's pattern of movement corresponds to that of a sexual encounter: first the pressing urgency of the approach to the beloved, suggested by insistent repetitions; then the ecstatic exclamations of the climax in stanza 5; followed by a relaxing of tension in the serenity and ultimate oblivion of the last three stanzas. His claim that "unless we respond to the sexuality the poem must fail of its full effect" seems amply justified; and his analysis can leave little room for doubt that San Juan experienced God in a quasi-sexual manner, that physical love was for him, in the words of Baruzi's own distinction, a symbol adhering directly to experience and not an analogy thought up at a later stage.

The "noche oscura" which the poem celebrates is in mystical terms the night of the senses, in which the brain no longer receives impressions from the outside world and the soul can apprehend reality directly, independently of the body. This freeing of the soul from its physical shackles is beautifully represented by the figure of the girl stealing out at dead of night from her hushed house. The concentration of this part of the poem is not unlike that of *cancionero* verse. There is insistent repetition – lines 3 and 5 of stanza 2 repeat those of stanza 1, "dichosa" occurs in each of the first three stanzas, "guiaba" echoes the "guía" of two lines earlier – and an almost obsessive emphasis on darkness and on the secrecy which this affords: "una noche oscura", "sin ser notada", "a escuras y segura", "la secreta escala", "a escuras y en celada", "la noche dichosa", "en secreto, que nadie me veía", "sin otra luz . . . ", "en parte donde nadie parecía". Dámaso Alonso comments on the density achieved by the scarcity of verbs. The first three stanzas contain only one main verb, "salí". That is the one important action: all the rest is exclamations of joy, or adverbial phrases reiterating the manner and circumstances of the flight (*11*, pp. 183–6).

All is dark, but the soul is led by an inner light burning within it. The paradox of light in darkness is not so sharp here as in some other poems, since the night itself is not luminous; yet the opposition is there in the opening lines – "oscura . . . inflamada" – and is reinforced when a light brighter than noonday blazes out in stanza 4, between two stanzas both beginning with a mention of night.

In all this first half of the poem there are only two concrete nouns, "casa" and "escala"; both form part of the same image of escape. Knowing how the poet did once escape from prison in the dark, letting himself down by means of an improvised rope, one is tempted to see a personal reminiscence here; but this must remain speculative, since the testimonies disagree as to whether this poem dates from before or after the escape. In his *Noche oscura* commentary San Juan tells only of the symbolic significance of the ladder or staircase. Cirlot's *Dictionary of Symbols* defines steps as a means of communicating with and breaking through to a higher level of being, and for San Juan too the ladder, although it can also serve for going down, for the descent into humility, is chiefly a means of upward access to God. Here the exegesis distorts the simple picture of the poem, and is scarcely any more helpful for its appreciation than the ensuing suggestion that the soul's "disfraz" consists of the white, green and red garments of faith, hope and charity (II, Chapters 18–21; *1*, pp. 710–21).

The girl meets her lover in the fourth stanza, but in an unspecified place – "adonde me esperaba . . . " – and referring to him only

as "quien yo bien me sabía". This allusive language matches the
secrecy of her venture, and on a different level echoes the "Que bien
sé yo" of *La fonte,* suggesting the mystic 'knowing' of something
that cannot be encompassed in a name. Stanza 5 with its threefold
apostrophe marks the culmination of the praise of night, as it does of
the lovers' union. Male and female become one, the soul is transformed into the very substance of God.

Night having done its priestly work then fades from the picture.
Hints of colour enter the poem, with "pecho florido", "cedros" and
"azucenas". The girl's relaxation into tranquillity is marked by a
succession of main verbs, as concentration is dissipated in gentle
movement and a returning awareness of her surroundings. Concrete
objects similarly abound in these last three stanzas: breast, hair, neck
and face; battlements, cedars and lilies. Stanzas 6 and 7 above all are
full of that sense of liberation and enrichment referred to at the
beginning of this chapter. The claustrophobic darkness is replaced
by "el aire del almena". *Tras de un amoroso lance* had also conveyed
an atmosphere of airiness and space, but here there is a horizontal
expansiveness too in the range of verbs and nouns and the sense
impressions they describe. The senses, left sleeping in the house at the
beginning of the poem, now return to register the wafting of the
cedars and the breeze fondling the girl's neck; even though its caress
suspends them again in a new and different kind of trance.

Repeated readings have not diminished my own emotional
response to this poem as they have in the case of the *Pastorcico.* If I
analyse this response, I find that it centres chiefly on two words,
"almena" and "azucenas". "Almena" delights me first by its complete unexpectedness. It occurs unremarkably in Córdoba's poem,
following naturally from the climbing of a tower; but nothing in
San Juan's earlier stanzas had prepared one for anything as concrete
or specific as battlements. Lilies are less alien to the atmosphere of
what has gone before; it has already been observed that "entre las
azucenas" is a borrowing from a similar love scene in the *Song of
Songs.* Yet the word is not inevitable, or foreseen, and it produces a
peculiar thrill when one meets it in the last line. The final stanza has
been moving back into abstractions as the girl gradually falls asleep.
There is a soporific quality about the repeated "-éme" endings, and a
laziness in the slack rhythm of "cesó todo y dejéme" and the indolent

repetition of "dejar". Then when one expects nothing more comes the bonus of "las azucenas", to round off stanza and poem with a visual image of great beauty and a line of perfect rhythmic flow.

The Arabic origin, in whole or in part, of both words gives them a certain exoticism, and may be another factor causing them to stand out as focal points in the poem. Certainly "azucenas" has for me a magic that "lirios" would not have had, and that is not in any way related to Garcilaso's use of the same word in a famous sonnet. Their chief power, however, probably lies in their function as indices marking the final downward movement of the poem. The girl begins by leaving all earthly reality behind her, in the single-mindedness of her venture. Her union with her lover transports her to the heights, to the airy battlements. Afterwards, in the lassitude of fulfilment, she sinks to earth again; but earth is no longer hidden in the excluding darkness, it is fertile and enriched with lilies. Lilies moreover are the emblem of purity. In this way San Juan uses the shorthand of his imagery to convey one of the paradoxes of mysticism: that though the mystic can only achieve the spiritual marriage by shutting out the world, after it the world is restored to him, transfigured and pure; nature, in Hatzfeld's phrase, is "otorgada a la novia como regalo nupcial" (*7*, p. 361).

Llama de amor viva

A note preceding the commentary to this poem states that its unusual metre (a modified *lira* made up of six lines of 7, 7, 11, 7, 7, 11 syllables respectively and rhyming a b c a b c), was taken from one of the versions *a lo divino* of Boscán. This is useful proof that San Juan was familiar with the work of Sebastián de Córdoba; though the poem in question is by Garcilaso, not Boscán, and is actually written in much longer stanzas, the first six lines of which follow the pattern indicated. As has been seen, one of the translations of Jacopone da Todi offers another possible source for San Juan's use of the metre.

As with *Noche oscura* verbal borrowings are not hard to trace: "esquiva" from the Todi translations (*15*, p. 131), "rompe la tela" from Garcilaso, probably via Córdoba, "llama de amor viva" from Córdoba's "fuego de amor vivo", "lámparas de fuego" perhaps from the *Song of Songs* VIII, 6, which in the Vulgate runs "lampades eius lampades ignis atque flammarum" (*11*, pp. 44–5, 83–6, 156–7). But again the fact of the borrowings is of minor importance; the words acquire renewed poetic significance in their conjunction in a perfectly integrated new lyric.

The whole of the short poem is this time given detailed theological exegesis in the corresponding commentary, but the literary critic does not need to refer to it often; response to the poem's symbolic fabric will carry him much further. Again there are two major symbols. The opening lines present a vivid, blazing image of sexual love; and the last stanza also describes a love scene, of a rather quieter kind. Yet apart from the "querido" of stanza 3 no actual persons are mentioned; the female is explicitly the soul, and the masculine element is a living flame, torches of fire. Thus the "llama sabrosa" which figured in a minor gloss is here developed into a symbol of burning and light which dominates the greater part of the poem, and gives new life to the old Petrarchan image of love as a fire. Some of the terminology of love in this poem is surprisingly trite: "esquiva", "dulce encuentro", "me enamoras"; but the flame penetrating to the centre of being speaks an altogether different language.

Nowhere else in San Juan's poetry is there such a piling-up of paradoxes: "tiernamente hieres", "cauterio suave", "regalada llaga" and the death-blow that brings life, as well as the light in darkness which here follows more appropriately than ever from the symbol of burning. Lamps, as the commentary points out, give both light and heat, and the soul's inner recesses being thus illuminated, themselves become incandescent enough to radiate both back to their source. The "profundas cavernas" are explained by San Juan as the three powers of the soul, memory, understanding and will: a narrow scholastic interpretation, and a poor exchange for the *frisson* of the dark caverns; but it does serve to make clear that "sentido" this time is not the senses, but the essence of sentient being itself. The torches blazing in the "profundas cavernas" are the other aspect of the flame tenderly searing the "más profundo centro" of the soul.

The paradox here, and in the "cauterio suave" and "regalada llaga", is very different from the Petrarchist posture of the lover who suffers but welcomes his suffering for its purifying and ennobling effects. Here there are contradictory elements in the actual sensation of contact, which is both wounding and tender, piercing and caressing. From the beginning there is as much of gentleness in the union as of passion, and the last stanza is all gentleness, from the "manso y amoroso" of its first line to the "delicadamente" of its last.

There is then some progression in this poem, though it is by no means as clearly defined as in the narrative of the *Noche oscura.* All its verbs but two are in the present tense. It opens *in medias res,* with the moment of consummation. The soul can ask for nothing more, unless it is for any further threat of hindrance to be removed by death. "Rompe la tela de este dulce encuentro" suggests a number of associations not irrelevant to mysticism: the veil of the Jewish temple (which kept worshippers out of the Holy of Holies) being rent in twain; the penetration of physical union; a textile in which the warp and the weft, starting as separate threads, have been woven into a single fabric. But while any of these ideas may enrich one's appreciation of the image, the only logical meaning it can have in its context here is the classical cutting of the thread of life. "Romper la tela" signifies this in the Garcilaso passage which San Juan may be echoing (see p. 46), and his own commentary is quite explicit: "Rompe la tela delgada de esta vida y no la dejes llegar a que la edad y años naturalmente la corten, para que te pueda amar desde luego con la plenitud y hartura que desea mi alma, sin término ni fin" (*Llama de amor viva,* Canción primera, 36; *I*, p. 1006).

Three of the poem's four stanzas express the rapture of union, thus corresponding to stanza 5 of the *Noche oscura;* and much of their language is similarly exclamatory and ecstatic. Few phrases are more than a line long, and some are mere gasps of joy. But though there is this time no gradual build-up to a climax, two verbs in the past tense do give an indication of the dead, dark state that went before. And though the final slackening of tension is less marked than in the *Noche,* some such relaxation is nevertheless suggested by the tenderness of the last stanza, and by the way in which no fewer than four pairs of words — "oscuro y ciego", "calor y luz", "manso y amoroso", "bien y gloria" — are coupled together to slow down the pace. Fire has faded out of the last stanza; love no longer strikes and wounds but dwells gently in the bosom, its "aspirar sabroso" recalling the voluptuous breezes on the battlements. But if the episode in the *Llama* has no beginning, neither is there any finality. The verb "morar", and the present tenses maintained to the last word of the poem, convey a sense of serene continuity, not unlike that of many of the lyrics of Luis de León.

The patterns of the two poems are thus similar but not identical. The *Noche* records the complete course of a mystical experience, the *Llama* only its middle phases; that is, the rapture itself and the beginnings of a return to tranquillity. The *Llama* could thus be said to correspond to stanzas 5, 6 and 7 of the *Noche*. Both poems use the symbol of sexual love, and each links it with another symbol of at least equal force: night dominates the first part of one poem, burning that of the other. These correspond, however, to the first and second phases of the experience, and fade from their respective poems as ecstasy yields to serenity, represented by the tenderness of human love.

The *Cántico espiritual,* or *Canciones entre el alma y el Esposo,* is the only long poem by San Juan de la Cruz. It consists of 39 stanzas (40 in Version B), in strict *lira* metre. Like the *Noche* and the *Llama* it records different stages in the mystic's experience, though its shape is not as clearly defined as that of either of the shorter poems. In its first eleven stanzas the soul is searching in anguish for the Beloved whom she has known and lost. She finds him again in stanza 12, and the rest of the poem is a dialogue in which the couple celebrate their love. There is no climax, and no clear movement from ecstasy to tranquillity. The intensity appears to fluctuate, and it has often been suggested that one reason for the re-ordering of some of the stanzas in Version B, whether by the poet himself or by a later hand, was precisely to give the poem a more logical progression and show a clear transition from the *desposorio* to the *matrimonio espiritual.*

As far as Version A is concerned, it seems unlikely that it was conceived as a single unit. It was certainly not written as such, since the testimonies of San Juan's nuns make it plain that he brought out of prison only 31 stanzas, up to and including that beginning "¡Oh ninfas de Judea! "; and that the last five were written later when he was established as confessor in the convent of Beas. Nothing is known about the composition of stanzas 32–4, but they may have been added last of all to link the other two sections together.

It is doubtful whether even the Toledan part of the poem was composed at a stretch. The love duet has a continuity about it suggesting that it could have been prolonged indefinitely, and it is not difficult to read it as a kind of diary of San Juan's continuing mystical experiences in prison. There is, on the other hand, a marked discontinuity between stanzas 12 and 13. Immediately after the appearance of the Beloved the soul sings a description of him in broad expansive phrases – "Mi Amado, las montañas . . . " – which hardly suggests the moment of union, and seems like the opening of a new poem. Duvivier, who has enquired closely into the genesis of the *Cántico,* thinks that stanzas 1–11 may have been composed

after 12–31 (though of course still during the imprisonment), in a
conscious attempt to give some shape to the work by contrasting the
bliss of union with the tortured state that went before (*17*, p. 133).

The *Cántico espiritual* is based on the biblical *Song of Solomon*,
or *Song of Songs*. This is a fragmentary work, a collection of Jewish
wedding songs of widely differing dates, the words of which are
sometimes put into the mouth of the bridegroom, sometimes of the
bride. It had traditionally been interpreted as an allegory of the love
between God and man and, since St Bernard wrote his sermons *In
cantica canticorum* on it in the twelfth century, had been a common
subject for meditation in the religious orders. San Juan must have
known it by heart to be able to draw on it as heavily as he does,
writing in prison and without the text in front of him. He does not
follow it systematically, there being in fact no system there to follow;
his reminiscences are haphazard. But it is to the *Song of Songs* that
he is indebted for the concept of a dialogue between spouses, for
the pattern of separation, search and reunion, and above all for the
voluptuous oriental atmosphere that characterizes much of his poem.
The gardens and scents, the flowers and fountains that form the
background to the nuptials, all come straight from his biblical original.

Other influences have also been traced. The questing soul's appeal
to the things of nature and her inability to find God in them are
related by the poet himself to St Augustine (*Cántico* Commentary,
1, pp. 851–3). A comparable passage in the *Confessions* is well
known,[13] but Marcel Bataillon has found still closer parallels in the
Soliloquia, writings attributed to Augustine but actually apocryphal,

[13]The passage is from Book X, Chapter 6: "'And what is this God? I asked
the earth and it answered: 'I am not He'; and all things that are in the earth
made the same confession. I asked the sea and the deeps and the creeping
things, and they answered: 'We are not your God; seek higher.' I asked the
winds that blow, and the whole air with all that is in it answered: 'Anaximenes
was wrong; I am not God.' I asked the heavens, the sun, the moon, the stars,
and they answered: 'Neither are we God whom you seek.' And I said to all the
things that throng about the gateways of the senses: 'Tell me of my God, since
you are not He. Tell me something of Him.' And they cried out in a great
voice: 'He made us.' My question was my gazing upon them, and their answer
was their beauty." (*The Confessions of St Augustine*, translated by F. J. Sheed,
London, 1960, p. 170)

which themselves already drew on the *Song of Songs*. [14] The fact that this part of the poem has evident non-biblical antecedents is one of Duvivier's reasons for differentiating it from the rest of the stanzas written in Toledo.

The role of classical and Renaissance influences in the *Cántico* has been a matter of some controversy. Dámaso Alonso, much of whose study of San Juan has been devoted to tracing the different poetic traditions underlying his verse, quotes several instances of apparent fusion. For example the hair that captivates the Lover in stanza 22 is a clear echo of the *Song of Songs* IV, 9, [15] but Alonso also links it with the second quatrain of Garcilaso's sonnet "En tanto que de rosa y azucena" where the words "cabello", "vuelo" and "cuello" similarly occur, and with the Petrarchist conceit of the hair as a snare or bond, as well as with popular Castilian verse. "Así se engarzan los influjos en San Juan de la Cruz" (*11*, pp. 36, 141, and 252 note 18). A little earlier María Rosa Lida, in an impressive study of San Juan's image of the wounded stag, had related this to Virgil, Horace and numerous of their Renaissance imitators, to the Galician-Portuguese lyric, and to Christian associations with the death of Christ, thus seeing in it a dense interweaving of biblical, classical and traditional symbolism, and a deliberate use of pagan ornamentation in a mystical context (*14*).

These views have been opposed by E. Setién de Jesús María, in his polemical work already referred to (see p. 31); by E. Allison Peers, who will allow only one fairly certain borrowing from Garcilaso ("El aspirar del aire,/el canto de la dulce Filomena", from lines 1146 and 1147 of Garcilaso's Second Eclogue, "el viento espira,/ Filomena sospira en dulce canto") (*16*); and more recently and more cogently by José L. Morales. Surprisingly enough it was not until this critic undertook the task in 1971 that anyone went to the trouble of making a detailed, line-by-line study of San Juan's bor-

[14]Marcel Bataillon, *Varia lección de clásicos españoles* (Madrid, 1964), pp. 170 ff.

[15]The Vulgate, which would be the version known to San Juan, reads: "Vulnerasti cor meum in uno oculorum tuorum et in uno crine colli tui." Other translations, including that by Luis de León, speak of a necklace rather than a hair. The Authorized Version has: "Thou has ravished my heart with one of thine eyes, with one chain of thy neck".

rowings from the *Song of Songs*. Having done so Morales concludes
that it is not necessary to postulate any classical or Renaissance
source for the *Cántico espiritual:* the commentary acknowledges no
such debts; and it is in any case unlikely that the Saint's earlier
reading or education would have been of the kind to enable him to
lay pagan and profane poetry under contribution in the isolation of
his prison cell (*18*, pp. 242–3).

Morales's caution is wise. Nevertheless a reader with even the
most superficial knowledge of Garcilaso who meets in the *Cántico* a
line like "Oh cristalina fuente", or who sees "Oh daughters of
Jerusalem" rendered as "Oh ninfas de Judea", will surely detect
Renaissance echoes. San Juan's borrowings from Córdoba in other
poems seem to be adequately substantiated, and there can be little
doubt that whatever his knowledge of Renaissance love poetry he
was thoroughly steeped in the *poesía a lo divino* which uses the
same forms, language and images and the same pastoral convention.
Orozco makes the point that among the features of the *Song of
Songs* not taken over by San Juan are those that stamp it as poetry
of an urban civilization: the references to streets and houses, doors
and windows, clothing and jewellery (*15*, pp. 209–13). He perhaps
exaggerates the contrast, since the biblical poem does also include
rural elements, and San Juan speaks of walls and thresholds; but in
general his comment on the subtle change of atmosphere is a valid
one. The *Cántico* is closer to nature and to pastoral. Its exoticism,
pervading as it is, is less intense than that of the *Song of Songs:* its
air is fresher and less heavy with perfumes; it has much less physical
sensuality, and more of the refined sensibility that characterizes
Garcilaso's Eclogues. Whatever the truth about precise verbal borrowings, Dámaso Alonso is surely right to suggest that in the *Cántico*
"se quiere como evocar ligeramente un ambiente rústico conocido y
próximo: evocarlo como reprimiéndolo a un tiempo mismo, para
que sólo reavive, y no sumerja, el ambiente original" (*11*, p. 145).
The refashioning of remote oriental love songs into a completely new
poetic creation remains the outstanding fact; but the transformation is due in some measure at least, directly or indirectly, to the
Renaissance lyric poets of Italy and Spain.

San Juan's commentary on the *Cántico espiritual,* like that on the
Llama, expounds its poem stanza by stanza; and many critics, particu-

larly those chiefly interested in his thought and doctrine, have
held that it is not possible to understand the poem without reference
to the poet's own exegesis. It is however a mistake to think of the
two as an indissoluble unit. Even Morales, who argues vehemently
that mystical poetry cannot be studied "de esta ladera", that is,
without full awareness of and sympathy with its spiritual content,
still emphasizes that the poem existed before the commentary, and
that there would never have been a commentary if the Madre Ana de
Jesús had not happened to ask for it; and moreover that the commentary was not intended as a clarification for the general reader,
but rather as a guide to enhance the value of the poem as devotional material for those already well advanced in the spiritual life
(*18*, pp. 77–9). San Juan's exegetical method is not to try to
explain or recapture the creative process, but rather to approach the
poem almost like the work of another person, and read new allegorical meanings into it. In fact, in the same way as much of his poetry
is *divinización* of previously existing verse, so much of the *Cántico*
commentary is a kind of 'contrafactum', of words which originally
conveyed their truth by poetic means. While it does at times clear
up obscurities, at others it can block the imaginative response that
would lead more directly to an understanding of the real sense. In
the words of L. J. Woodward, "the easy escape to the commentary,
'to find what the poem means', has prevented most of us from
paying attention to the poem".[16] Since in this study I aim above all
to pay attention to the poem, I shall refer to the commentary,
as to the *Song of Songs,* only when there seems to be good reason for
doing so.

The symbol of sexual love which shares the honours in the *Noche*
and the *Llama* fills the whole of the *Cántico espiritual.* The verbs
"escondiste", "dejaste" and "huiste" in the first three lines indicate
an opening *in medias res:* the lovers have been together and he has
wounded or stricken her with love, but now he is hidden from her
and she must go out in search of him. This is San Juan's poetic

[16]Review of Jorge Guillén, *Language and Poetry,* in *Bulletin of Hispanic
Studies,* XXXIX (1962), 103.

account of the 'dark night of the soul', in which the mystic who
has had isolated experiences of union with the divine ceases for a
time to recapture them, and suffers acutely until they return. This
stage of the 'mystic way' is so graphically described by San Juan in
his *Noche* commentary that it is surprising to find it recorded only
twice in his verse: in the gloss on "Vivo sin vivir en mí", and much
more poignantly and dramatically in this opening section of the
Cántico. The language of the first stanza is very simple, the only
figurative elements being the conventional wound of love and the
simile of the stag. This latter derives from the "roe or young hart"
to which the lover is three times likened in the *Song of Songs,* but it
is also rich in other associations. Whether or not there are classical
influences at work here, María Rosa Lida is almost certainly right to
point to the connotations of meek suffering which in the Middle Ages
made the stag a figure of Christ. Cirlot listing it as one of the symbols
in his *Dictionary* states that it was sometimes depicted with a cross
between its antlers, and that at other times these represented the
branches of the Tree of Life. San Juan's "ciervo" suggests therefore
not merely the speed of the Lover's flight, but also his divine nature
and self-sacrificing love.

The girl in the *Song of Songs* asks the night watchmen in the city
for news of her beloved, the soul here appeals to shepherds who may
be climbing the hill to the sheepfolds. The words "pastores",
"majadas" and "otero" establish at an early stage the pastoral background of the poem. The shepherds are to tell the one whom she
describes, with characteristic imprecision, as "aquel que yo más
quiero", of her suffering and pain. This she voices in three verbs of
increasing intensity: "adolezco, peno y muero". Orozco, who of all
San Juan's critics is probably the most alert to the auditory qualities
of his verse, points out how the $e - o$ assonance of the verb endings
reinforces the insistence of the repetition (*15,* p. 51).

Plaintiveness yields to single-minded determination in the much
more resolute verbs of stanza 3: "iré . . .ni cogeré . . . ni temeré . . .
y pasaré . . . ". The poetic play of rhythm and sound is very marked
here, in the stress patterns of the verbs and the alliteration of "flores",
"fieras", "fuertes y fronteras", which also calls attention to these
important words. The flowers are the enticements along the way,
and the commentary interprets the last three as the temptations of,

respectively, the world, the devil and the flesh (*1*, pp. 750–1). But a more natural response would surely be to see fortresses and frontiers as man-made obstacles to progress, and flowers and wild beasts as contrary manifestations of nature: its distracting delights and its menacing untamed forces, including those of the physical passions.

Having thus introduced the theme of nature in relation to the 'mystic way' San Juan explores it further in the next four stanzas. Following St Augustine he makes the soul seek for God among the meadows and groves, but seek in vain. The woods were planted by the Beloved, he has passed through them again and his mere glance has clothed them with beauty, but the halting, imperfect account they give of him – the stammering effect of "un no sé *qué que quedan* balbuciendo' has often been noted – leaves the soul so frustrated that she bursts out in another cry of pain: " ¡Ay! ¿quién podrá sanarme? "

A sudden switch of her restless mind then turns her attention back within herself. There are *cancionero* echoes in the paradox and polyptoton of "oh vida, no viviendo donde vives", followed by an image of unusual complexity:

> y haciendo porque mueras
> las flechas que recibes
> de lo que del Amado en ti concibes.

Even the syntax here is involved, and this is one of the few points in the poem where the actual sense of the words, as opposed to their deeper associations, is at all difficult to unravel. There is a double movement from without to within: something of the Beloved is conceived within the soul, who then herself manufactures this vague, formless "lo" into piercing arrows that again penetrate and kill her. In mystical terms, it is not God who inflicts the suffering of the 'dark night', it is the soul who, remembering past happiness in present misery, can only re-experience it as a sharp pain.

The symbolism here is much stronger than the rather trite love talk of heart and eyes that follows. Yet it is the eyes that lead back to the outside world, and to the most dramatic moment of the poem. The soul gazes into a crystal spring and longs to see her Lover's eyes reflected there. The sudden miracle happens, and she does see them. The fountain, says San Juan, is faith, and "llámala cristalina a la fe . . .

porque es de Cristo su Esposo" (*1,* p. 762). The verbal association
is an obvious and natural one; but the "cristalina fuente" is also a
common feature of pastoral poetry. Dámaso Alonso traces its possible ancestry in love scenes in the Second Eclogue of Garcilaso and
the rendering *a lo divino* by Sebastián de Córdoba (*11,* pp. 40–2,
67–8); he might perhaps also have adduced the opening of
Nemoroso's song in the First Eclogue, where trees gaze at their
reflection in "aguas puras, cristalinas". And the fountain has here
too all the associations of a life-giving force that attached to it in the
Fonte que mana y corre. In the first ten stanzas of the *Cántico* the
soul alludes half a dozen times to sickness or death. After the
fountain has restored her Lover to her she does not mention them
again, and the rest of the poem is full of the richness of life.

The sight of the beloved eyes is at first too much for her to bear
and she soars aloft in her ecstasy. She is again a bird on the wing, not
this time a hunting hawk but a tender dove. The Lover is again the
stag, this time specifically a "ciervo vulnerado", whose wounds of
love are soothed by the cool breeze created by her flight.

With the reunion of the lovers the mood and even the language
structure changes. There is little further action. Dámaso Alonso has
observed how verbs become much fewer, and how on the other hand,
in contrast to the rather spare language of the opening, an outpouring of nouns and adjectives makes for a great richness of sense
impressions. The adjectives moreover have a full part to play. Unlike
Garcilaso who so often preceded his nouns with epithets so appro-
riate and expected as almost to form a single unit of sense with the
noun – "blanco pie", "claro arroyo", "dulce primavera" – San Juan
extends his nouns by means of succeeding adjectives which start
long trains of associations (*11,* pp. 190–4).

Stanzas 13–26 are the love song of the Bride. She begins by
describing her Beloved in terms of the things of nature: mountains,
valleys and rivers, remote islands, languorous breezes. The commentary at this point is as evocative and as beautiful as the poem
itself, and expounds the first two lines better than any critic could:
"Las montañas tienen alturas, son abundantes, anchas, hermosas,
graciosas, floridas y olorosas. Estas montañas es mi Amado para mí.
Los valles solitarios son quietos, amenos, frescos, umbrosos, de dulces
aguas llenos, y en la variedad de sus arboledas y suave canto de aves

hacen gran recreación y deleite al sentido, dan refrigerio y descanso en su soledad y silencio. Estos valles es mi Amado para mí" (*1*, p. 769).

The sense of hearing is very present in these stanzas: the rivers are sonorous and the breezes sigh; and if these phrases verge on the trite, the same cannot be said about the paradoxes of stanza 14. Other mystics have described their experiences in similar auditory terms; there is a parallel for San Juan's "música callada" in Eliot's "music heard so deeply that it is not heard at all", and an even closer one in Emily Brontë:

> Mute music soothes my breast, unuttered harmony . . .
>
> (*The Complete Poems of Emily Jane Brontë*,
> ed. C. W. Hatfield, New York, 1941, No.190)

It seems clear that in such phrases he is not finding equivalents for God, but recording something of the actual manner of his mystical awareness.

Finally comes one of those totally unexpected lines that counteracts the lulling effect of sonorous nature and makes one alert to the full implications of the imagery: "la cena que recrea y enamora". "Cena" is a word with strong Christian associations of life-imparting sacrificial love, and these are inevitably evoked here. But the commentary only mentions the more homely idea of supper as the reward for a hard day's work, and the beginning of rest. There is too, although Morales does not take it up, a mention of a love feast in the *Song of Songs:* "He brought me to the banqueting house, and his banner over me was love" (II, 4). Full of meanings as the phrase can be shown to be, its poetic force lies not least in its sheer unexpectedness at this point.

These two memorable *liras* in which the soul ranges in imagination through nature in order to describe her Beloved seem to constitute the core of the poem. As relatively early a critic as Baruzi noted the apparent contradiction that whereas before the things of nature could only reflect God and stammer out something inadequate about him, now they *are* God; or rather God is them. But the two apprehensions are not alike. One derives from a sentimental pantheism, the other leads us to a kind of vision of the essence of things (*4*, p. 348). More recently Gerald Brenan has pointed to the same paradox (*5*, p. 132), and to San Juan's own resolution of it in the *Llama* commentary: the need to "conocer por Dios las criaturas, y no por las criaturas a Dios" (*1*, p. 1087). The experience of God gives an altogether new life and meaning to nature, just as it clothes the earth with lilies at the end of the *Noche oscura*. It is worth noting too that although the soul proposed to range "por esos montes y riberas" in her search for the Beloved, the creatures she questioned were familiar, earth-bound meadows and thickets; the soaring mountains and the distant isles far exceed these in might and mystery.

Stanzas 15–17 are heavy with imagery from the *Song of Songs*, and topics suggested by it follow each other in rapid succession: the marriage bed, decked with royal purple and gold and hedged about with the dens of strong and kingly lions; the chorus of virgins all enamoured of the Bridegroom; and the intoxicating vapours of the spiced wine. Here the biblical text allows San Juan to develop a mystical symbol that seems at first incongruous: drunkenness, imply-ing alienation from self and from former rational awareness. It was an image belonging particularly to oriental mystical traditions: Happold quotes instances of its use by Sufi and Islamic mystics (*20*, pp. 97–8). San Juan himself comes near to it in the "tan embebido,/ tan absorto y enajenado" of one of his glosses, but this moment in the *Cántico* brings the most explicit use of it in his verse. The "in-terior bodega" of the Beloved is, like the fountain springing in the dark, the centre and source of life. After entering and drinking from it the soul "cosa no sabía" – as in the "Entréme donde no supe/y quedéme no sabiendo" of the gloss – and her drunkenness is even realistically suggested by the concentration of thick consonants in "a*dob*a*d*o", "*b*álsamo", "*b*o*d*ega" and "*b*ebí".

Then comes a return to pastoral imagery, as she implies her changed state by saying that she has lost her sheep and no longer tends a flock. The echoes here, says Dámaso Alonso, may be classical, but are more probably from the many popular *villancicos* which link falling in love with the abandonment of sheep (*11*, pp. 137–8). The unexpected metaphor of a game is next introduced: the soul "se hace perdidiza", loses herself deliberately, throws herself away like a pawn in order to be won by her 'opponent'. All through this part of the poem the images shift rapidly in an impressionistic manner, fos-tering a sense of unreality and dream. In one line the Bridegroom is experienced as an electrifying touch — "toque de centella" — and in the next as heady wine. The soul who began as a royal bride is suddenly a shepherdess — whether a genuine peasant or a figure from Arcadia it is not quite clear — and then a pawn on a chessboard.

There is a similar strangeness about the arresting line "De flores y esmeraldas" which opens stanza 21. To weave garlands of flowers plucked in the cool of the morning is a natural enough occupation for lovers, but are these real emeralds interwoven with them? The commentary is unhelpful, merely explaining them as divine gifts, and there are no emeralds in the *Song of Songs*. Cirlot gives a possible clue when under the heading 'Grail' he shows how the emerald comes to represent eternity. Since the garland is a bond, a symbol of fellowship, a garland containing emeralds would betoken an eternal union. But this is to allegorize, and lose the thrill of the surprising juxtaposition.

The love idyll continues with some of the very few physical details borrowed from the *Song of Songs:* the hair blowing round the neck, the eye, and the dark complexion. All the eroticism has gone, however; there is none of the sensual delight in lips, breasts and thighs, and the only significance of the soul's beauty is that she has received it from the Beloved. Just as "mil gracias derramando" he had looked on natural objects and "vestidos los dejó de hermosura", so now his look has imprinted "gracia y hermosura" on her. Human nature and inanimate nature are thus linked in their relationship to and dependence on God.

The soul ends her aria with more biblical echoes: the little foxes, the flowering vineyard, the winds blowing over the garden and the Beloved feeding among the flowers. These are not random elements, however. They seem to have been brought together from different parts of the *Song* in order to build up two impressions which are to govern much of the rest of the poem. The first is that of the static setting. There is no shifting impressionism now: from stanzas 21 to 31 the lovers are plainly in a garden. The word "flores" or its derivatives occurs five times in this passage, "huerto" twice, there are two mentions of scents, two of roses, and one of an apple tree. And secondly the garden, like that of the *Song,* is enclosed. It is a secret, private place; not, as in the Freudian symbolism of the biblical text, the bride herself, but the bridal chamber. Cirlot defines 'garden' as nature subdued, ordered and enclosed; as a female precinct; and as a scene of conjunctions. Disturbing intrusions are to be warded off, therefore, and images are chosen, and even manipulated, to emphasize this: where the biblical poet calls both the north wind and south wind to fan the scents in the garden, San Juan denies entry to the "cierzo muerto", as to the foxes that threaten the vines.

The fragrant breezes and the grazing among the flowers (lilies in the *Song of Songs*) link the last stanza of the soul's monologue with the end of the *Noche oscura,* and similarly suggest a descent into oblivion. As she drowses the Bridegroom takes up the echoes of "el rostro recliné sobre el Amado" with "el cuello reclinado/sobre los dulces brazos del Amado", and hushes all the things of nature so that the bride may sleep undisturbed. The invocatory list of stanza 29, ranging through living creatures, landscapes and the elements of water, air and fire, inevitably recalls the description of the Beloved himself as some of these very things — mountains, valleys, waters and winds — at the moment of reunion. It is almost as though there has been a return to an earlier stage where the things of creation are inimical to spiritual satisfaction. Once again, however, as with the "cena que recrea y enamora", a startling last line, quite unrelated to the quintessential "aguas, aires y ardores", brings experience back to a human level. The "miedos de las noches veladores" have their origin in the *Song of Songs* III, 8, but their inclusion in the general cosmic adjuration ends the *lira* on an unexpected note, like a sudden modulation into a new key.

The last two stanzas San Juan wrote in prison are very close to the biblical text, with their notion of a walled garden whose privacy must be preserved; yet in the words "liras", "sirenas" and "ninfas" they also contain a remarkable concentration of classical-Renaissance elements. The "ninfas de Judea" represent the closest intermingling of the two main poetic currents present in the *Cántico espiritual.*

By now the soul has taken up the strain again, and her two stanzas are followed by two more from the Bridegroom and then a final coda of five from the soul. But as in the *Song of Songs* it is more a question of alternation than of real dialogue. The lovers do not converse with each other, they sing in turn, each dwelling on the theme of secrecy and withdrawal. The notion of solitude occurs in the dominant position in every line of the Bridegroom's last stanza.

The bride repeatedly invites her lover to seclusion, to silence and to secret explorations.

In the last eight strophes, added at a later date, the setting has changed again. It is no longer the garden but somewhere more broad and spacious, like the background of a Raphael or a Leonardo paint-ing – or like the landscape of the earlier part of the poem. Mountains, shores and strange islands reappear, rushing water and caverns among rocky heights. And yet all this is mysteriously one with penetration into dark and hidden depths. The poem so far has been constructed on an outward and an inward movement. The soul went out in search of her lover, and ranged through creation until she found him. Then after her brief ecstatic flight the images were all of inwardness: the encircled marriage bed, the inner wine cellar, the walled garden. Now at the end of the poem the two movements have become one; the hidden caves are lofty, and to climb the mountain is to pene-trate the thicket. Stanzas 35 and 36 are San Juan's supreme poetic account of the mystical paradox of a spaciousness which is also seclusion.

Other elements previously encountered recur in these post-Toledan stanzas: the dove, the wound of love, the gift by the Beloved of a vague "aquello", and the ever-present breeze. And there are echoes of other poems too, in the spring of pure water, the calm night and the flame that consumes without pain; so that these verses composed in Beas, perhaps the last the Saint ever wrote, become a résumé of some of his major themes.

If the introductory stanzas give progression to the poem by drama-tizing the transition from one phase to another, in the *envoi* too there are brief backward glances recalling the passage from turmoil to tranquillity. The dove brings the olive branch back to the Ark after the havoc of the Flood, and in the closing lines a siege is lifted. The past tenses here distance this final stanza from the rest of the poem, which has all been actualized in the present, and bring the long episode to a conclusion. The *Cántico* began like the *Noche oscura* with a "salí", and it ends like it too with a descent. In the longer poem, however, it seems clear that the opening and closing sections have been added later, to give overall shape to a work in the main body of which there is no temporal progression.

Nothing in the whole poem is more evocative than the image of the horsemen which brings it to an end. Gerald Brenan, with his own knowledge of Andalusia to draw on, sees in it the memory of centuries of frontier fighting, and a string of horses or mules winding peacefully down to the river after the skirmishing is over. "In these last two wonderful lines, with their gently reassuring fall, the horses descending within sight of the waters are lifted out of time and made the symbol of the peace of this land of eternal recurrence" (*5*, p. 115). This serene picture seems much closer to the sense of the verse than Hatzfeld's reading of "la caballería" as "el esplendor militar, la más refinada tentación de la gloria mundana basada en la guerra" (*7*, p. 367); even though Morales also insists (*18*, p. 234) that this is military cavalry, deriving from the "chariots of Amminadib" in the *Song of Songs* VI, 12.

For once San Juan's own elucidation is perhaps the one that draws the most satisfying meaning from his image. In the closing paragraphs of the commentary he explains "la caballería" as the lower part of human nature, more specifically the senses, and the waters as manifestations of God (both traditional symbolic roles). The horses come within sight of the water. They can never go right down and drink of it since the senses cannot encompass God, but they can come within its influence and receive from it "recreación y deleite" (*1*, pp. 828–9). This beautiful final image thus epitomizes what in a way the whole poem has been about: the sanctification of the senses through the mystical experience. As channels to mediate God to the soul they were almost useless, but once he is known mystically they can become the means whereby his oneness with all reality may be expressed. The whole fabric of the poem is sensuous, but only because the broad vistas and sounding waters, the garden scents, the taste of the wine and the touch of the breeze have all been brought within the sphere of the divine, and, after the exaltation is over, remain peacefully near the deep waters of everlasting being.

All the stages of the 'mystic way' are recorded in the major poems of San Juan de la Cruz: the 'night of the senses' and an isolated experience of union in the *Noche oscura;* a similar single ecstasy in the *Llama de amor viva;* and the 'dark night of the soul' followed by the enduring 'spiritual marriage' in the *Cántico espiritual.* Only one common feature of mystical life is lacking, the outgoing aspect of the final phase in which there is a renewal of activity on behalf of others. Right to the end of the *Cántico* the outside world is excluded: "Que nadie lo miraba . . . " This is not to suggest that San Juan's religion was an affair of spiritual self-indulgence, merely to point to the absence from the poems themselves of anything corresponding to Eckhart's descent from the seventh heaven to take water to his sick brother, or to Teresa's "entre los pucheros anda el Señor". Most of his verses in any case originated in solitary confinement when questions of practical activity did not arise. They were composed in privacy as well as in privation, and the mystical songs among them are totally private.

Like most mystical writings their concerns are not moral. There is no "Domine non sum dignus", no questioning of the soul's right to enjoy God. Sin is something scarcely even alluded to, much less felt as an obstacle; and if there has in the past been a struggle against evil, as the mention of Aminadab (the Devil) implies, it has now long since ceased.

To fight the good fight is an essential part of Christianity, and this lack of a moral dimension is what most separates San Juan's poems from the central Christian tradition. Apart from the probable Christian associations in the symbols of the supper and the stag, in all three major poems there is only one reference to sin and redemption. This comes in stanza 28 of the *Cántico:* "Debajo del manzano . . .": God's marriage with the soul restores to the daughter the honour lost by her mother Eve. But this is a simple borrowing from the *Song of Songs* VIII, 5, which in the Vulgate runs: "Sub arbore malo suscitavi te, ibi corrupta est mater tua, ibi violata est

genitrix tua', and from traditional exegeses linking the tree of Eden
with the tree of the Cross; it has little real affinity with the substance
of the poem. The absence of Christian nomenclature is also striking.
The soul never speaks of "Cristo" or even of "Dios", only of her
"Amado" or, less precisely still, "aquel que yo más quiero", or
"quien yo bien me sabía". Unlike the raptures of Santa Teresa,
who frequently saw visions of Christ, those of San Juan seem not
to have been tied to the Christian revelation. Although he naturally
equated their object with the God of his beliefs, as the commentaries
make plain, he belongs to the broad universal tradition of mysticism
whose awareness is of total reality, infinite love, or some ultimate
essence to which it is scarcely possible to give a name.

Even in his non-mystical and explicitly Christian poems human
sinfulness has a very small part to play. His *Romances* on the
Creation and Incarnation surprisingly omit all reference to the Fall.
The Son comes down to earth not as redeemer, but simply through
an overflowing of divine love. The *Pastorcico* allegorizes what is in
Christian terms the supreme encounter between good and evil, but
even it says very little about man's guilt in the matter − merely
that the Shepherd is "olvidado de su bella pastora" who does not
want his company. All the emphasis again is on love. Although the
sincerity and intensity of San Juan's religious beliefs cannot possibly
have been called in question, it is not difficult to understand how in
an age obsessed by heresy the one-sidedness of his presentation of
Christianity may have provoked some uneasiness among his superiors.

When to this playing down of the struggle with sin is added the
comparatively brief treatment of the 'dark night of the soul' − only
at most seven *liras* from the beginning of the *Cántico* express any
real anguish − the impression received is of a deliberate minimizing
of any sense of strain; and the question must arise whether San Juan's
verse is not altogether too lacking in tension, too effortless and
dulcet. What, if anything, lifts it above the level of a rather sickly
devotionalism and makes it great poetry?

Of no small importance is his mastery of his craft and in particular
his smooth handling of rhythm. In all the fifty-one *liras* of his three
major poems there are no more than six or seven ungainly lines.
His one technical failing is the occasional recourse to an unnecessary
"ya" to make up the syllable count; and this only obtrudes when it

occurs in too many lines in succession, as in stanzas 19—20 of the *Cántico*. Other evidence of his craftsmanship has already been seen in the ways he manipulates earlier verse, blending different kinds of material in a fully integrated new poem, or deftly turning a love lyric into a perfect vehicle for mysticism. It is not known how much polishing and re-writing he did. In addition to the two main versions of the *Cántico* in the MSS of Sanlúcar and Jaén there are minor variants in other MSS, and it seems likely that the poems underwent a number of small changes in repeated readings before being committed to writing in the versions that have become established. Be that as it may, for a man who was neither a professional poet nor in touch with literary activity apart from the regular versifying in the religious houses, his skill is impressive.

Even more so is what Hatzfeld calls his "estilo paradójico-evocativo" (7, p. 372): the unexpected details and the surprising juxtapositions, whether of normally incompatible opposites like darkness and brightness, secrecy and space, or of unrelated elements such as flowers and emeralds, which work by poetic means to shock the mind into response. Here San Juan's isolation from literary circles was probably a benefit to him, since it left him unhampered by the principle of literary decorum: the idea that there were rules for writing, and that to depart from the norms was to produce a bad work. For Garcilaso it is right and proper that streams should be clear, meadows green and women golden-haired, and any individualizing or unexpected note would have jarred on his hearers. This is the classical ideal of beauty, and it can produce works greatly satisfying in their harmony and 'rightness', in literature as in architecture or sculpture. But it will sometimes pall, and provoke truancies and reactions of the kind soon to be dared by Quevedo and Góngora. San Juan does not react against classical decorum, he ignores it; and so, though his poems still have many of the same accepted "hermosuras" as those of Garcilaso, he is also able to produce the thrill of the stylistic "no sé qué que se alcanza por ventura".

Though much of his natural imagery is of the kind familiar from Renaissance verse he does not by any means follow all the conventions of the latter. For all his dwelling on brightness there is no mention of the sun, moon or stars so beloved of the Petrarchists. Objects, even flowers, are not usually described in terms of their colours; in the

whole of his poetry the only colours explicitly mentioned are the
"verduras" of the meadow and the purple and gold of the royal
marriage bed. (In fact for a poet who is known from his surviving
drawings to have had artistic talent the degree of clear visualization
in his imagery seems surprisingly small; the other senses play at least
as important a part.) Whatever is borrowed, from whatever source,
is taken over not for any reason of 'public' acceptability but only
because it is significant for the poet himself. As Gerald Brenan says:
"No poet borrowed more from other poets, yet none was more
original, because before he began to write all the work of trans-
mutation into his own categories had been accomplished" (*5*, p. 125).
This complete adequation of his poetic material to its new purpose
is one of the great strengths of his verse.

Its mystical content does not, as has occasionally been suggested,
raise his poetry to a level of creation where literary criticism becomes
impertinent, but neither is it a negligible factor in its impact. It gives
the poems an honesty and an authenticity to which any sensitive
reader must respond in some measure. And it makes its own
peculiarly poetic contribution to the literature of mysticism through
the attention paid in the major poems to the role of the senses. If
there is a feeling of liberation in these poems it is not merely because
nature has been introduced as a background and the vocabulary and
range of impressions correspondingly widened, but also because the
senses, and by implication the whole of man's earthly nature, have
indeed been freed by the mystical experience and allowed to share in
that awareness of transcendent reality to which they were formerly
a hindrance. The sense impressions in San Juan's poems are making
an important statement about the mystic's rediscovery of the world,
now transfigured; the reverse of the neoplatonism of Luis de León,
who is still striving to "know God through the creatures".

At the same time many of these sense impressions also have a
symbolic value. The *Cántico* is full of the names of objects. Some
of these are taken over from the *Song of Songs* with little or no
additional meaning, others belong to the realm of what Cirlot calls
explicit symbolism: a kind of iconographic shorthand, based on the
generally recognized significance attached to certain objects, and
interpreted on an intellectual level. Thus when San Juan writes "el
mosto de granadas gustaremos" he is echoing the *Song of Songs* VIII,

2: "I would cause thee to drink of spiced wine of the juice of my pomegranate"; but he probably also has in mind the accepted meanings of the pomegranate indicated by Cirlot: "reconciliation of the multiple and diverse within apparent unity", "a symbol of the Oneness of the universe".[17] Other objects again are true symbols in the archetypal sense, and it is probably through these that San Juan's poetry makes its most universal appeal.

Duvivier stresses this factor: "l'imagination de Jean de la Croix passe par les archétypes, tout comme sa poésie doit se soumettre à la figuration par la nature et accueillir des formes et thèmes d'expression traditionnels: il est assez grand mystique et assez vrai poète pour user des ressources de l'inconscient à la manière dont il use de l'univers objectif ou des procédés littéraires hérités de ses prédécesseurs" (*17*, p. 487).[18] From these subconscious resources come the sexuality of the three major poems, the image of night which has impressed so many critics, and a number of other figurative elements that have received less attention but are still clearly rich in significance. Two groups of these may be identified. The first comprises the bright flame; the river or fountain as source of life; the air or breeze with its connotations of spirit, and of love ("el silbo de los aires amorosos", "austro que recuerdas los amores"); and the mountain, well characterized by María Rosa Lida as "tangencia de cielo y tierra donde se

---

[17]This is suggested by the commentary, which at this point adheres so closely to the actual image as to make it seem likely that the idea was in the poet's mind from the beginning, and not read in at a later stage: "Así como las granadas tienen muchos granicos, todos nacidos y substentados en aquel seno circular, así cada virtud y atributo y misterio y juicio de Dios contiene en sí gran multitud de granos de efectos y ordenaciones maravillosas de Dios, contenidos y substentados en el seno esphérico o circular de virtud y misterio que pertenece a aquellos tales efectos. Y notamos aquí la figura circular o esphérica de la granada, porque cada granada entendemos aquí por una virtud y atributo de Dios; el cual atributo o virtud de Dios es el mesmo Dios, el cual es significado por la figura circular o esphérica, porque no tiene principio ni fin" (*1*, p. 218).

[18]"The imagination of John of the Cross feeds on the archetypes, just as his poetry has to submit to the imagery of nature and employ traditional forms and modes of expression: he is a great enough mystic and a true enough poet to use the resources of the subconscious in the same way as he uses "the objective universe or the literary procedures inherited from his predecessors."

cumplen todas las epifanías" (*14,* p. 49). These images, representative of the four elements of fire, water, air and earth, suggest the cosmic nature of San Juan's fundamental symbolism, and typify the wide-ranging, out-reaching aspect of his verse. The second group, in contrast, are images of inward penetration: the wine cellar, the walled garden, the hidden caves. They symbolize the mystical centre, Teresa's "Interior Castle" and Eckhart's "Seelengrund", or base of the soul, which is at once the seat and the source of being. Cirlot links the various myths of the centre with medieval alchemy: "the dream of the 'subterranean sun' shining at the bottom of the alchemist's oven like the light of salvation within the depths of the soul" (p. xxix). It is not difficult to relate this picture to the flame and the fountain also in some of their manifestations: the lamps of fire blazing in the deep caverns, and the hidden fountain springing in the night.

Georges Morel points to San Juan's frequent use of the word "centro" in the commentaries, and helps to elucidate the ideas connected with it. The centre, like that of a rotating sphere, is motionless, the point of rest towards which all activity tends. But since there is constant motion towards it the centre also becomes the limit towards which one strives. "L'homme progresse au sein de l'univers métaphysique semblable au navire qui fend les eaux par sa proue . . . L'homme qui vit à la pointe de son être vit par là même comme un être 'centré', acquérant équilibre dans ce déséquilibre . . . L'idée de fond, qui indique, comme l'idée sanjuaniste de centre, une limite extrême, impose en effet aussi l'idée d'ampleur: aller au fond c'est aller au bout" (*9,* Vol. II, p. 289).[19] In this way the voyaging and the penetration become one, and the hidden caverns are rightly situated at the mountain tops.

The poetry of San Juan de la Cruz, built so largely out of paradox, is itself paradoxical in being the most private of its age through the nature of its inspiration and the circumstances of its composition,

---

[19]"Man moves towards the heart of the metaphysical universe like a ship cleaving the waters with its prow . . . The man who lives at the extreme point of his being lives, by that same fact, as a 'centred' being, acquiring balance in this imbalance . . . The idea of the depths, which implies, like San Juan's idea of the centre, an uttermost point, also in fact imposes the idea of distance: to go to the depths is to go to the limit."

and at the same time the most universal through the timeless validity of its symbols. The poet stands to one side of the general line of development of Golden Age verse. He had no influence on later poets, to whom even his existence was probably unknown. When his poems were first published in the seventeenth century it was as the basis for his commentaries, and for three hundred years he was considered only as a theologian. It has been left to the present century to discover his poetry. Dámaso Alonso made clear its literary qualities thirty years ago, but readers of the present day may well prove to be more fully in tune than any previous generation with its mystical absorption in transcendent reality and its awareness of the deep significance of creation.

Bibliographical Note

The great majority of writers on San Juan de la Cruz, a high proportion of them Spanish and French, have been interested in him chiefly as a religious writer and have concerned themselves with the commentaries rather than the poems. For a full bibliography up to a fairly recent date see Pier Paolo Ottonello, *Bibliografia di San Juan de la Cruz* (Edizioni del Teresianum, Rome, 1967), which contains over 2,000 items. The same author has also published a "Bibliographie des problèmes esthétiques et littéraires chez San Juan de la Cruz" in *Bulletin Hispanique,* LXIX (1967), 123–38. The following very selective list is limited to works with a substantial bearing on the poems.

EDITIONS

The poems have almost invariably been published either in conjunction with the commentaries or extracts from them, or as appendices to works of criticism.

1. *Vida y obras de San Juan de la Cruz.* Biografía por el R. P. Crisógono de Jesús, revisión del texto póstumo del P. Crisógono y notas críticas por el R. P. Matías del Niño Jesús, prólogo general, edición crítica de las obras del doctor místico, notas y apéndices por el R. P. Lucinio del SS. Sacramento. Biblioteca de Autores Cristianos, 4th ed., Madrid, 1960.

   The most useful working text, providing in one manageable volume the definitive biography, a scholarly edition of the complete works including the different versions of the commentaries, and full textual apparatus.

2. *Poesías completas de San Juan de la Cruz y comentarios en prosa a los poemas,* ed. Dámaso Alonso and Eulalia Galvarriato de Alonso, Colección Crisol, 3rd ed., Madrid, 1968.

   A handy small volume, though unfortunately not without printing errors. Only selections from the commentaries are included.

3. *Cántico espiritual,* ed. M. Martínez Burgos, Clásicos Castellanos, Madrid, 1924, reprinted 1952.

   The Jaén version of poem and commentary. The Introduction is entirely devoted to arguing the superiority of this version.

GENERAL STUDIES

4. Baruzi, Jean. *Saint Jean de la Croix et le problème de l'expérience mystique.* 2nd ed., Paris, 1931.

   A major pioneer work, not without literary relevance, although the main approach is psychological and metaphysical.

5. Brenan, Gerald. *St John of the Cross. His Life and Poetry.* Cambridge, 1973.

A polished and readable account, mainly of the life. The 36 pages on the poetry draw on Dámaso Alonso, but also contains some valuable new insights.

6.   Gicovate, Bernard. *San Juan de la Cruz.* Twayne's World Authors Series 141. New York, 1971.
        A largely biographical introductory study. The analysis of the poems is sensitive, if not searching.

7.   Hatzfeld, Helmut. *Estudios literarios sobre mística española.* 2nd ed., Madrid, 1968.
        A collection of previously published articles, including some close and revealing analyses of San Juan's style in both prose and poetry.

8.   Milner, Max. *Poésie et vie mystique chez Saint Jean de la Croix.* Paris, 1951.
        An unoriginal but useful survey.

9.   Morel, Georges. *Le Sens de l'existence chez Saint Jean de la Croix.* 3 vols, Paris, 1960–1.
        Vol. III, *Symbolique,* is largely devoted to the poems, and is the only extensive study of their symbolism.

10.   Peers, E. Allison. *Studies of the Spanish Mystics.* Vol. I, London, 1927.
        Chapter V is on San Juan, with 14 pages on his major poems. A little rhapsodic, but with some close observations that pointed the way for later criticism.

THE POEMS

11.   Alonso, Dámaso. *La poesía de San Juan de la Cruz (desde esta ladera).* Madrid, 1942.
        The first and still the most important analysis of San Juan's poetic style.

12.   Alonso, Dámaso. *Poesía española. Ensayo de métodos y límites estilísticos.* 4th ed., Madrid, 1962.
        One essay, "El misterio técnico en la poesía de San Juan de la Cruz", repeats some sections of *11* and revises others in the light of later discoveries.

13.   Jones, R. O. *A Literary History of Spain. The Golden Age: Prose and Poetry.* London, 1971.
        An excellent survey of the whole period with five very perceptive pages on San Juan's major poems.

14.   Lida, María Rosa. "Transmisión y recreación de temas grecolatinos en la poesía lírica española", *Revista de Filología Hispánica,* I (1939), 20–63.
        An important study of the traditions behind the symbols of the stag and the fountain.

15. Orozco, Emilio. *Poesía y mística. Introducción a la lírica de San Juan de la Cruz.* Madrid, 1959.
     A collection of articles constituting a major contribution to the study of San Juan's poetry.

16. Peers, E. Allison. "The alleged debts of San Juan de la Cruz to Boscán and Garcilaso", *Hispanic Review,* XXI (1953), 1–19, 93–106.
     An unconvincing attempt to refute Dámaso Alonso's statements on the influence of the Renaissance poets and Sebastián de Córdoba.

THE CÁNTICO ESPIRITUAL

17. Duvivier, Roger. *La Genèse du "Cantique spirituel" de Saint Jean de la Croix.* Paris, 1971.
     The long, detailed study of the genesis of both poem and commentary includes incidentally many valuable literary observations.

18. Morales, José L. *El "Cántico espiritual" de San Juan de la Cruz: su relación con el "Cantar de los Cantares" y otras fuentes escriturísticas y literarias.* Madrid, 1971.
     Establishes for the first time San Juan's precise debts to the *Song of Songs.* Very good where factual, though assessment of previous critics is somewhat vitiated by an anti-literary bias.

TRANSLATION

19. Campbell, Roy. *The Poems of St John of the Cross.* London, 1952. Reprinted in Penguin Classics, Harmondsworth, 1960.
     The Spanish text with a verse translation; probably the most satisfactory rendering in English.

A GENERAL WORK ON MYSTICISM

20. Happold, F. C. *Mysticism.* Harmondsworth, 1963.
     An excellent survey, followed by an anthology of extracts from mystical writings.